Crock Pot Creations Culinary Adventures

Flavorful Recipes with Stunning Photos

By Ida Carroll

Copyright © by Ida Carroll

All rights reserved. No part of this publication may be reproduced, distributed, or transmitted in any form or by any means, including photocopying, recording, or other electronic or mechanical methods, without the prior written permission of the publisher, except in the case of brief quotations embodied in critical reviews and specific other noncommercial uses permitted by copyright law.

This book is a work of authorship by Ida Carroll and is offered to the public for personal and noncommercial use only. The recipes, content, photographs, and illustrations contained within are the property of the author and the publisher and are protected under the United States and international copyright laws.

The information in this book is presented in good faith, but no warranty is given, nor are results guaranteed. The publisher and author disclaim any liability concerning the use of this information. Recipes and contents will be used at your discretion, considering personal dietary needs and restrictions.

The trademark "Crock Pot" is used herein for descriptive purposes only and does not imply endorsement or affiliation with the trademark owner. The term "Crock Pot" in this publication merely indicates the general cooking style and does not refer to any specific brand or product.

While every effort has been made to ensure the accuracy of the information herein, the author and publisher cannot be held responsible for any errors, omissions, or inconsistencies. The views and opinions expressed in this book are solely those of the author and do not necessarily reflect those of the publisher.

Introduction

Welcome to "Crock Pot Creations: Culinary Adventures," a gastronomic journey masterfully crafted by Ida Carroll. This book is not just a collection of recipes; it's an invitation to explore the art of slow cooking, savor each flavor, and create unforgettable meals with ease and confidence.

Step into a world where cooking is not just a chore but a delightful experience. "Crock Pot Creations" offers 50 authentic and original recipes, each meticulously tested to ensure perfect flavors that will tantalize your taste buds. This cookbook transforms the humble crock pot into a culinary canvas where magic unfolds one recipe at a time.

Divided into five mouth-watering chapters - Meat, Chicken, Vegetarian, Fish and Seafood, and Soup - each section presents ten unique recipes. These dishes aren't just meals but adventures in flavor, color, and texture. From the hearty meat dishes to the light and flavorsome seafood recipes, every palate and preference is catered to. The vegetarian chapter bursts with fresh, vibrant ingredients, while the soups offer comfort and warmth, perfect for any season.

Each recipe in this book comes to life with original, colorful photographs, ensuring you see precisely what you can create. The standard color printing in the paperback edition enhances the visual appeal, making it a feast for the eyes. The easy-to-follow instructions ensure that even novice cooks can produce exquisite results. Imagine the pride and joy of serving dishes that look as good as they taste every single time.

Begin your culinary adventure with "Crock Pot Creations." Whether you're a seasoned chef or a beginner, this cookbook is your perfect companion in the kitchen. Experience the joy of cooking confidently from flawlessly tested recipes, clear instructions, and stunning photography. Embark on this flavorful journey and transform your meals into culinary creations. Your crock pot is waiting to unveil its potential; let "Crock Pot Creations" guide your culinary adventure!

Table of Contents

Chapter 01: Savory Meat Alternatives 7
- Recipe 01: Roast Beef With Large Chunks of Beef 7
- Recipe 02: Beef Pot Roast and Vegetables 9
- Recipe 03: Beef Stew 11
- Recipe 04: Goulash or Beef Stew 13
- Recipe 05: Roast Beef and Potatoes 15
- Recipe 06: Beef Chowder With Vegetables 17
- Recipe 07: Meatballs Casserole 19
- Recipe 08: Irish Stew With Tender Lamb Meat 21
- Recipe 09: Short Beef Ribs With Potatoes 23
- Recipe 10: Kentucky Burgoo Stew 25

Chapter 02: Poultry-Free Delights 27
- Recipe 11: Whole Juicy Chicken 27
- Recipe 12: Chicken Stuffing Casserole 29
- Recipe 13: Mississippi Chicken Breasts 31
- Recipe 14: Stewed Chicken Breast With Mushrooms 33
- Recipe 15: Chicken Cacciatore 35
- Recipe 16: Stewed Chicken Breast With Mushrooms 37
- Recipe 17: Pulled Chicken 39
- Recipe 18: Stewed Chicken With Rice and Dates 41
- Recipe 19: Chicken Stew With Vegetables 43
- Recipe 20: Chicken Tinga 45

Chapter 03: Verdant Veggie Varieties 47
- Recipe 21: Mushroom and Potato Stew 47
- Recipe 22: Stewed Cabbage Potato 49
- Recipe 23: Fried Cassava 51
- Recipe 24: Carrot and Celery Stew 53
- Recipe 25: Pilaf With Chick-Pea and Mushrooms 55

Recipe 26: Vegetarian Crock Pot Chili..57
Recipe 27: Halves of a Butternut Squash....................................59
Recipe 28: Young Potatoes Sprinkled With Dill............................61
Recipe 29: Curry With Black Lentils and Red Kidney Beans..........63
Recipe 30: Zucchini, Tomatoes, Bell Pepper and Garlic Stew.......65

Chapter 04: Ocean-Inspired Eats..67
Recipe 31: Cod Fillet With Greens Steamed...............................67
Recipe 32: Fish Soup With Grilled Polenta..................................69
Recipe 33: Garlic Prawns...71
Recipe 34: Shrimps or Prawns in Garlic Olive Oil.........................73
Recipe 35: Seafood Crock Pot...75
Recipe 36: Mussels in Crock Pot..77
Recipe 37: Fish Stew in Crock Pot..79
Recipe 38: Prawn, Squids, Fish and Mussels..............................81
Recipe 39: Salmon Fish Broth..83
Recipe 40: Salmon With Spinach and Teriyaki Sauce..................85

Chapter 05: Soothing Soup Sensations................................87
Recipe 41: Chicken Vegetable Soup...87
Recipe 42: Gazpacho Soup..89
Recipe 43: Red Lentil Vegetable Soup..91
Recipe 44: Beef, Vegetable, and Tomato Soup...........................93
Recipe 45: Pearl Barley Beans Soup...95
Recipe 46: Turmeric Split Pea Soup..97
Recipe 47: Mushroom Barley Soup...99
Recipe 48: Chicken Soup With Dumplings................................101
Recipe 49: Veal Stew Soup..103
Recipe 50: Soup With Beans, Tomato and Bread......................105

Chapter 01: Savory Meat Alternatives

Recipe 01: Roast Beef With Large Chunks of Beef

Savor the classic comfort of a hearty "Roast Beef with Potatoes and Carrots," a crock pot recipe that effortlessly combines succulent large chunks of beef with the wholesome goodness of potatoes and carrots. This dish is a timeless favorite, perfect for those who appreciate the simplicity and richness of slow-cooked meals.

Servings: 6

Prepping Time: 20 mins

Cook Time: 8 hours

Difficulty: Easy

Ingredients:

- 2 lbs beef roast
- 4 large potatoes, cut into chunks
- 4 carrots, cut into chunks
- 1 onion, chopped
- 3 cloves garlic, minced
- 2 cups beef broth
- 1 tbsp Worcestershire sauce
- Salt and pepper to taste
- Fresh herbs for garnish (like rosemary or thyme)

Step-by-Step Preparation:

1. Place the beef roast in the crock pot.
2. Surround the beef with potatoes, carrots, onion, and garlic.
3. Pour in beef broth and Worcestershire sauce. Season with salt and pepper.
4. Cook on low for 8 hours until the beef is tender and vegetables are cooked.
5. Garnish with fresh herbs before serving.

Nutritional Facts: (Per serving)

- Calories: 450
- Carbohydrates: 35g
- Protein: 40g
- Fat: 18g
- Fiber: 5g
- Sodium: 300mg

This "Roast Beef with Potatoes and Carrots" epitomizes home-cooked comfort. It's a simple yet satisfying meal that fills your home with inviting aromas and brings warmth to any dinner table.

Recipe 02: Beef Pot Roast and Vegetables

Relish the rich and hearty flavors of "Beef Pot Roast and Vegetables," a classic crock pot dish that epitomizes comfort food. This recipe slowly simmers beef to tender perfection alongside a medley of vegetables, creating a mouthwatering meal that's satisfying and easy to prepare.

Servings: 6

Prepping Time: 15 mins

Cook Time: 8 hours

Difficulty: Easy

Ingredients:

- 3 lbs beef chuck roast
- 3 carrots, chopped
- 2 onions, quartered
- 3 potatoes, cubed
- 4 cloves garlic, minced
- 2 cups beef broth
- 1 tbsp olive oil
- 1 tsp dried rosemary
- 1 tsp dried thyme
- Salt and pepper to taste

Step-by-Step Preparation:

1. Sear beef is roasted in olive oil until browned on all sides.
2. Place the roast in the crock pot.
3. Add carrots, onions, potatoes, and garlic around the roast.
4. Pour beef broth and sprinkle with rosemary, thyme, salt, and pepper.
5. Cook on low for 8 hours until the beef is tender.
6. Serve the roast with the vegetables.

Nutritional Facts: (Per serving)

- Calories: 500
- Carbohydrates: 20g
- Protein: 48g
- Fat: 25g
- Fiber: 3g
- Sodium: 400mg

Enjoy the simplicity and deliciousness of this "Beef Pot Roast and Vegetables," a dish that brings comfort and heartiness to any meal. Perfect for gathering around the table and enjoying the flavors of a well-cooked home meal.

Recipe 03: Beef Stew

Delve into the comforting embrace of "Beef Stew with Potatoes and Carrots in Tomato Sauce," a delicious crock pot creation. This recipe blends tender beef, hearty potatoes, and sweet carrots in a rich tomato sauce, resulting in a warm, flavorful stew perfect for any cozy meal.

Servings: 6

Prepping Time: 20 mins

Cook Time: 8 hours

Difficulty: Easy

Ingredients:

- 2 lbs beef stew meat, cubed
- 3 potatoes, cubed
- 3 carrots, sliced
- 1 onion, chopped
- 2 cups tomato sauce
- 2 cups beef broth
- 2 cloves garlic, minced
- 1 tsp dried thyme
- 1 tsp dried basil
- Salt and pepper to taste

Step-by-Step Preparation:

1. Place beef stew meat in the crock pot.
2. Add potatoes, carrots, and onion.
3. Pour tomato sauce and beef broth over the ingredients.
4. Add garlic, thyme, basil, salt, and pepper.
5. Cook on low for 8 hours until the beef is tender and vegetables are cooked.

Nutritional Facts: (Per serving)

- Calories: 350
- Carbohydrates: 30g
- Protein: 35g
- Fat: 10g
- Fiber: 5g
- Sodium: 500mg

Savor each bite of this "Beef Stew with Potatoes and Carrots in Tomato Sauce," a dish that perfectly captures the essence of home cooking. It's a satisfying, hearty meal that's sure to become a favorite at your family gatherings.

Recipe 04: Goulash or Beef Stew

Immerse yourself in the rich flavors of "Goulash or Beef Stew," a classic crock pot dish that's hearty and comforting. This traditional recipe combines tender beef, robust spices, and a medley of vegetables, slowly cooked to perfection, offering a taste of homely warmth in every spoonful.

Servings: 6

Prepping Time: 20 mins

Cook Time: 8 hours

Difficulty: Easy

Ingredients:

- 2 lbs beef chuck, cut into cubes
- 3 potatoes, diced
- 2 onions, chopped
- 2 carrots, sliced
- 2 cloves garlic, minced
- 3 cups beef broth
- 2 tbsp tomato paste
- 1 tsp paprika
- 1/2 tsp caraway seeds
- Salt and pepper to taste

Step-by-Step Preparation:

1. Place beef chunks in the crock pot.
2. Add potatoes, onions, carrots, and garlic.
3. Mix beef broth with tomato paste, paprika, and caraway seeds. Pour over the beef and vegetables.
4. Season with salt and pepper.
5. Cook on low for 8 hours until meat is tender.

Nutritional Facts: (Per serving)

- Calories: 380
- Carbohydrates: 25g
- Protein: 40g
- Fat: 15g
- Fiber: 4g
- Sodium: 600mg

Enjoy the comforting and fulfilling taste of this "Goulash or Beef Stew," a dish that brings the heartiness of a traditional meal to your table. It's the perfect recipe for a cozy night, offering warmth and deliciousness.

Recipe 05: Roast Beef and Potatoes

Indulge in the timeless classic, "Roast Beef and Potatoes," a crock pot dish that epitomizes comfort food at its finest. This recipe effortlessly combines succulent roast beef with hearty potatoes, slow-cooked to perfection, ensuring a tender, flavorful meal that will please any palate.

Servings: 6

Cook Time: 8 hours

Prepping Time: 15 mins

Difficulty: Easy

Ingredients:

- 3 lbs beef chuck roast
- 4 large potatoes, quartered
- 1 onion, sliced
- 2 cloves garlic, minced
- 2 cups beef broth
- 1 tbsp Worcestershire sauce
- Salt and pepper to taste
- Fresh herbs for garnish (like rosemary or thyme)

Step-by-Step Preparation:

1. Place the beef chuck roast in the crock pot.
2. Arrange potatoes and onion slices around the roast.
3. Sprinkle minced garlic over the meat.
4. Pour beef broth and Worcestershire sauce over the ingredients.
5. Season with salt and pepper.
6. Cook on low for 8 hours until the roast is tender.
7. Garnish with fresh herbs before serving.

Nutritional Facts: (Per serving)

- Calories: 500
- Carbohydrates: 20g
- Protein: 48g
- Fat: 25g
- Fiber: 3g
- Sodium: 500mg

"Roast Beef and Potatoes" is a simple yet sumptuous meal, ideal for a comforting family dinner or a cozy gathering. Its rich flavors and tender texture make it a beloved dish for all occasions.

Recipe 06: Beef Chowder With Vegetables

Dive into the hearty and comforting flavors of "Beef Chowder with Vegetables," a crock pot recipe that's a symphony of taste and texture. This dish combines tender beef with a vibrant mix of corn, celery, potatoes, and jalapeño, all enhanced with fresh thyme, creating a warming and satisfying meal perfect for any day.

Servings: 6

Prepping Time: 20 mins

Cook Time: 8 hours

Difficulty: Easy

Ingredients:

- 2 lbs beef stew meat, cubed
- 2 potatoes, diced
- 1 cup corn
- 2 stalks celery, chopped
- 1 onion, chopped
- 2 cloves garlic, minced
- 1 jalapeño, finely chopped
- 4 cups beef broth
- 1 tsp fresh thyme
- Salt and pepper to taste

Step-by-Step Preparation:

1. Place beef cubes in the crock pot.
2. Add diced potatoes, corn, celery, onion, garlic, and jalapeño.
3. Pour beef broth over the ingredients.
4. Sprinkle with fresh thyme, salt, and pepper.
5. Cook on low for 8 hours until beef is tender and vegetables are cooked.
6. Adjust seasoning as needed before serving.

Nutritional Facts: (Per serving)

- Calories: 350
- Carbohydrates: 25g
- Protein: 30g
- Fat: 15g
- Fiber: 4g
- Sodium: 500mg

This "Beef Chowder with Vegetables" is a delightful and nourishing dish, perfect for those chilly evenings or when you need a comforting and satisfying meal. Its rich flavors and hearty ingredients make it a sure favorite

Recipe 07: Meatballs Casserole

Immerse yourself in the homely and savory delight of "Meatballs Casserole," a crock pot masterpiece perfect for any meat lover. This recipe brings together juicy meatballs, rich sauces, and melty cheese, all slow-cooked to perfection, creating a comforting and irresistibly delicious dish.

Servings: 6

Prepping Time: 30 mins

Cook Time: 4 hours

Difficulty: Medium

Ingredients:

- 1 lb ground beef or turkey
- 1/2 cup breadcrumbs
- 1 egg, beaten
- 1 onion, finely chopped
- 2 cloves garlic, minced
- 1 jar marinara sauce
- 1 cup shredded mozzarella cheese
- 1 tsp Italian seasoning
- Salt and pepper to taste

Step-by-Step Preparation:

1. Mix ground meat, breadcrumbs, egg, half of the onion, and seasoning. Form into meatballs.
2. Place meatballs in the crock pot.
3. Pour marinara sauce over meatballs and sprinkle with remaining onion and garlic.
4. Cook on low for 4 hours.
5. Top with mozzarella cheese and cook until cheese melts.

Nutritional Facts: (Per serving)

- Calories: 350
- Carbohydrates: 18g
- Protein: 25g
- Fat: 20g
- Fiber: 2g
- Sodium: 500mg

Enjoy the rich and hearty "Meatballs Casserole," a perfect dish for family dinners or gatherings. Its flavorful profile and easy preparation make it a hit for any occasion, offering a comforting and satisfying meal.

Recipe 08: Irish Stew With Tender Lamb Meat

Immerse yourself in the rich, traditional flavors of "Irish Stew with Tender Lamb Meat," a crock pot dish that embodies the essence of Irish cuisine. This comforting stew blends succulent lamb with hearty vegetables, slow-cooked to perfection, offering a warm, nourishing, rustic, and satisfying meal.

Servings: 6

Prepping Time: 20 mins

Cook Time: 6 hours

Difficulty: Easy

Ingredients:

- 2 lbs lamb stew meat, cubed
- 3 potatoes, cubed
- 2 carrots, sliced
- 1 onion, chopped
- 2 cups beef broth
- 1 cup Guinness beer (optional)
- 1 tsp rosemary
- 1 tsp thyme
- Salt and pepper to taste

Step-by-Step Preparation:

1. Place lamb cubes in the crock pot.
2. Add potatoes, carrots, and onion.
3. Pour in beef broth and Guinness beer.
4. Season with rosemary, thyme, salt, and pepper.
5. Cook on low for 6 hours until lamb is tender and vegetables are soft.

Nutritional Facts: (Per serving)

- Calories: 400
- Carbohydrates: 30g
- Protein: 35g
- Fat: 15g
- Fiber: 4g
- Sodium: 300mg

Enjoy the authentic taste of Ireland with this "Irish Stew with Tender Lamb Meat," a dish that brings comfort and warmth to your dining table. It's a hearty meal that will delight family and friends, perfect for a cozy night in.

Recipe 09: Short Beef Ribs With Potatoes

Savor the rich and spicy goodness of "Short Beef Ribs with Potatoes in Spicy Sauce," a crock pot recipe that promises to tantalize your taste buds. This dish perfectly combines tender beef ribs with hearty potatoes, all smothered in a flavorful spicy sauce, creating an indulgent and satisfying meal.

Servings: 6

Prepping Time: 20 mins

Cook Time: 8 hours

Difficulty: Medium

Ingredients:

- 2 lbs short beef ribs
- 4 large potatoes, cubed
- 1 onion, chopped
- 2 cloves garlic, minced
- 2 cups beef broth
- 1 cup spicy BBQ sauce
- 1 tsp smoked paprika
- Salt and pepper to taste
- Fresh parsley for garnish

Step-by-Step Preparation:

1. Place short ribs in the crock pot.
2. Add cubed potatoes, onion, and garlic.
3. Pour in beef broth and spicy BBQ sauce.
4. Season with smoked paprika, salt, and pepper.
5. Cook on low for 8 hours until ribs are tender.
6. Garnish with fresh parsley before serving.

Nutritional Facts: (Per serving)

- Calories: 450
- Carbohydrates: 35g
- Protein: 30g
- Fat: 20g
- Fiber: 4g
- Sodium: 600mg

Indulge in this "Short Beef Ribs with Potatoes in Spicy Sauce" for a heartwarming meal. Its deep flavors and tender meat make it a perfect dish for any occasion, guaranteed to impress and satisfy your family and friends.

Recipe 10: Kentucky Burgoo Stew

Delve into the heart of Southern cooking with "Kentucky Burgoo Stew," a crock pot marvel known for its rich mishmash of meats and vegetables. This hearty stew is a celebration of flavors and textures, bringing together a variety of ingredients to create a comforting and satisfying meal that's perfect for any gathering.

Servings: 8

Prepping Time: 30 mins

Cook Time: 10 hours

Difficulty: Medium

Ingredients:

- 1 lb beef stew meat, cubed
- 1 lb chicken, cubed
- 1 lb pork shoulder, cubed
- 3 potatoes, diced
- 2 carrots, sliced
- 1 onion, chopped
- 2 cups corn
- 2 cups beef broth
- 1 can diced tomatoes
- 1 tsp paprika
- Salt and pepper to taste

Step-by-Step Preparation:

1. Combine beef, chicken, and pork in the crock pot.
2. Add potatoes, carrots, onion, and corn.
3. Pour in beef broth and add diced tomatoes.
4. Season with paprika, salt, and pepper.
5. Cook on low for 10 hours until meats are tender and flavors meld.

Nutritional Facts: (Per serving)

- Calories: 400
- Carbohydrates: 25g
- Protein: 40g
- Fat: 15g
- Fiber: 4g
- Sodium: 500mg

Enjoy the unique and delectable "Kentucky Burgoo Stew," a dish embodying Southern comfort food's spirit. It's perfect for a cozy night in or a festive gathering, offering everyone a warm and hearty experience at the table.

Chapter 02: Poultry-Free Delights

Recipe 11: Whole Juicy Chicken

Experience the simple yet delightful pleasure of a "Whole Juicy Chicken" cooked in a crock pot. This recipe ensures a succulent, flavorful chicken is effortlessly prepared and perfect for any occasion. Whether it is a family dinner or a special gathering, this dish guarantees a tender and juicy meal with minimal fuss.

Servings: 6

Prepping Time: 15 mins

Cook Time: 6 hours

Difficulty: Easy

Ingredients:

- 1 whole chicken (about 4 lbs)
- 1 onion, sliced
- 4 garlic cloves, minced
- 1 lemon, quartered
- 2 tsp paprika
- 1 tsp dried thyme
- Salt and pepper to taste
- Fresh herbs for garnish

Step-by-Step Preparation:

1. Place sliced onion at the bottom of the crock pot.
2. Season the chicken inside and out with paprika, thyme, salt, and pepper.
3. Stuff the chicken with lemon quarters and minced garlic.
4. Place the chicken in the crock pot.
5. Cook on low for 6 hours until the chicken is cooked through.
6. Garnish with fresh herbs before serving.

Nutritional Facts: (Per serving)

- Calories: 350
- Carbohydrates: 3g
- Protein: 40g
- Fat: 20g
- Sodium: 300mg

Relish the wholesome goodness of this "Whole Juicy Chicken," a testament to the joys of simple yet delicious cooking. It's a fuss-free, satisfying meal that brings comfort and flavor to your dining table.

Recipe 12: Chicken Stuffing Casserole

This Crock Pot Chicken Stuffing Casserole combines tender chicken with savory stuffing, creating a delicious meal with minimal effort.

Servings: 6

Prepping Time: 15 minutes

Cook Time: 4 hours

Difficulty: Easy

Ingredients:

- 4 boneless, skinless chicken breasts
- 1 package dry stuffing mix
- 1 cup chicken broth
- 1 can cream of chicken soup
- 1/2 cup sour cream
- 1/4 cup diced onions
- Salt and pepper to taste

Step-by-Step Preparation:

1. Place chicken breasts at the bottom of the Crock Pot.
2. Mix stuffing, broth, soup, sour cream, and onions in a bowl.
3. Spread the mixture over the chicken.
4. Cook on low for 4 hours.
5. Season with salt and pepper before serving.

Nutritional Facts: (Per serving)

- Calories: 350
- Protein: 25g
- Carbohydrates: 22g
- Fat: 15g
- Sodium: 650mg

Enjoy the comforting flavors of this Chicken Stuffing Casserole, a perfect dish for busy days or cozy evenings, ensuring a satisfying meal every time.

Recipe 13: Mississippi Chicken Breasts

Mississippi Chicken, a flavorful Crock Pot dish, combines chicken breasts with au jus gravy, ranch seasoning, butter, and pepperoncini peppers for a deliciously easy meal.

Servings: 6

Prepping Time: 10 minutes

Cook Time: 6-8 hours

Difficulty: Easy

Ingredients:

- 4 boneless, skinless chicken breasts
- 1 packet au jus gravy mix
- 1 packet ranch seasoning mix
- 1/2 cup unsalted butter
- 6-8 pepperoncini peppers

Step-by-Step Preparation:

1. Place chicken in the Crock Pot.
2. Sprinkle with au jus gravy mix and ranch seasoning.
3. Add pepperoncini peppers and place butter on top.
4. Cook on low for 6-8 hours.
5. Shred the chicken in the pot and mix well.

Nutritional Facts: (Per serving)

- Calories: 300
- Protein: 25g
- Carbohydrates: 5g
- Fat: 20g
- Sodium: 800mg

Mississippi Chicken is the perfect blend of tangy, savory, and comfort, making it an ideal dish for busy weekdays or relaxed weekend dinners.

Recipe 14: Stewed Chicken Breast With Mushrooms

Savor the taste of tender chicken breasts stewed with hearty mushrooms in this Crock Pot recipe. It's a simple yet delicious meal perfect for any day of the week.

Servings: 4

Prepping Time: 15 minutes

Cook Time: 6 hours

Difficulty: Medium

Ingredients:

- 4 boneless, skinless chicken breasts
- 2 cups sliced mushrooms
- 1 onion, chopped
- 2 cloves garlic, minced
- 1 cup chicken broth
- 1 tsp thyme
- Salt and pepper to taste

Step-by-Step Preparation:

1. Place chicken in the Crock Pot.
2. Add mushrooms, onion, and garlic.
3. Pour chicken broth over the ingredients.
4. Season with thyme, salt, and pepper.
5. Cook on low for 6 hours until chicken is tender.

Nutritional Facts: (Per serving)

- Calories: 165
- Protein: 26g
- Carbohydrates: 4g
- Fat: 4g
- Sodium: 300mg

Enjoy this Stewed Chicken Breast with Mushrooms, a delightful blend of flavors and textures, bringing warmth and comfort to your dining table.

Recipe 15: Chicken Cacciatore

Chicken Cacciatore, a classic Italian dish, is made easily with this Crock Pot recipe. Enjoy tender chicken simmered in a rich tomato sauce with vegetables and herbs, perfect for a comforting family meal.

Servings: 6

Prepping Time: 20 minutes

Cook Time: 8 hours

Difficulty: Medium

Ingredients:

- 4 boneless chicken breasts
- 1 can diced tomatoes
- 1 onion, chopped
- 2 bell peppers, sliced
- 3 garlic cloves, minced
- 1/2 cup chicken broth
- 2 tsp Italian seasoning
- Salt and pepper to taste

Step-by-Step Preparation:

1. Place chicken in the Crock Pot.
2. Add diced tomatoes, onion, bell peppers, and garlic.
3. Pour in chicken broth.
4. Sprinkle Italian seasoning, salt, and pepper.
5. Cook on low for 8 hours until chicken is tender.

Nutritional Facts: (Per serving)

- Calories: 220
- Protein: 27g
- Carbohydrates: 10g
- Fat: 7g
- Sodium: 410mg

Chicken Cacciatore in the Crock Pot offers a deliciously hearty and wholesome meal, bringing the flavors of Italy right to your table with minimal effort.

Recipe 16: Stewed Chicken Breast With Mushrooms

Indulge in the flavors of Stewed Chicken Breast with Mushrooms, a Crock Pot dish that combines succulent chicken and earthy mushrooms in a deliciously rich sauce. It's a perfect meal for those seeking comfort and simplicity in cooking.

Servings: 4

Prepping Time: 15 minutes

Cook Time: 6 hours

Difficulty: Easy

Ingredients:

- 4 boneless, skinless chicken breasts
- 2 cups of sliced mushrooms
- 1 diced onion
- 2 minced garlic cloves
- 1 cup chicken broth
- 1 teaspoon dried thyme
- Salt and pepper to taste

Step-by-Step Preparation:

1. Place chicken breasts in the Crock Pot.
2. Top with mushrooms, onion, and garlic.
3. Pour in chicken broth and sprinkle with thyme, salt, and pepper.
4. Cook on low for 6 hours until chicken is tender.
5. Stir gently before serving.

Nutritional Facts: (Per serving)

- Calories: 210
- Protein: 31g
- Carbohydrates: 5g
- Fat: 7g
- Sodium: 320mg

Enjoy this Stewed Chicken Breast with Mushrooms for a cozy and satisfying meal, a testament to the effortless art of slow cooking.

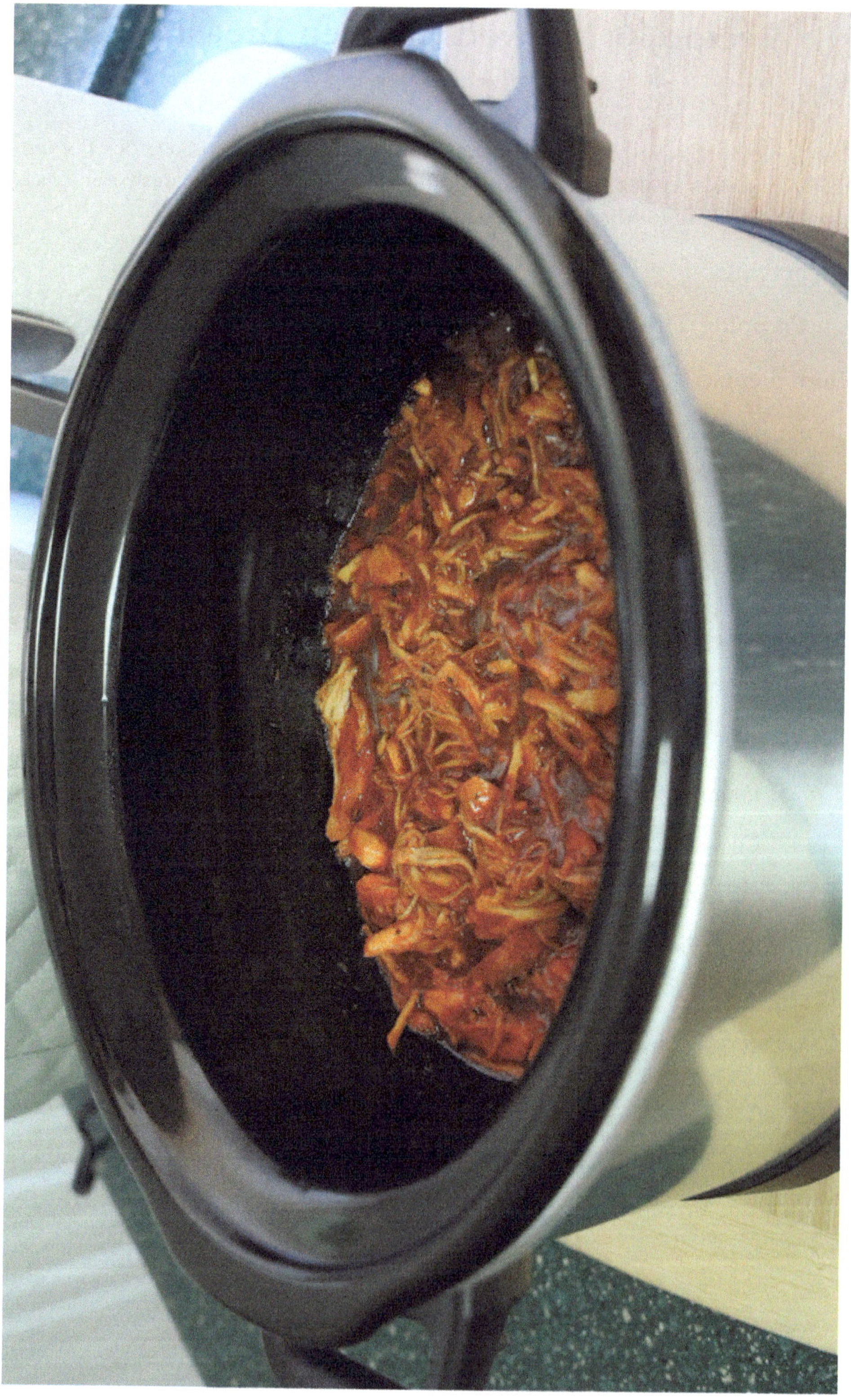

Recipe 17: Pulled Chicken

Delight in the simplicity and flavor of Pulled Chicken, a versatile Crock Pot dish that's both easy to prepare and deliciously satisfying. Tender, shredded chicken cooked in savory spices makes for an ideal meal any day of the week.

Servings: 8

Prepping Time: 10 minutes

Cook Time: 4-6 hours

Difficulty: Easy

Ingredients:

- 4 boneless, skinless chicken breasts
- 1 cup barbecue sauce
- 1/4 cup apple cider vinegar
- 1/4 cup brown sugar
- 1 tbsp Worcestershire sauce
- 1 tsp smoked paprika
- Salt and pepper to taste

Step-by-Step Preparation:

1. Place chicken breasts in the Crock Pot.
2. Mix barbecue sauce, vinegar, brown sugar, Worcestershire sauce, paprika, salt, and pepper in a bowl.
3. Pour the mixture over the chicken.
4. Cook on low for 4-6 hours.
5. Shred the chicken with forks and stir well.

Nutritional Facts: (Per serving)

- Calories: 220
- Protein: 25g
- Carbohydrates: 18g
- Fat: 4g
- Sodium: 480mg

Pulled Chicken from the Crock Pot is a mouth-watering, tender delight, perfect for sandwiches, salads, or as a main dish, making meal times effortless and enjoyable.

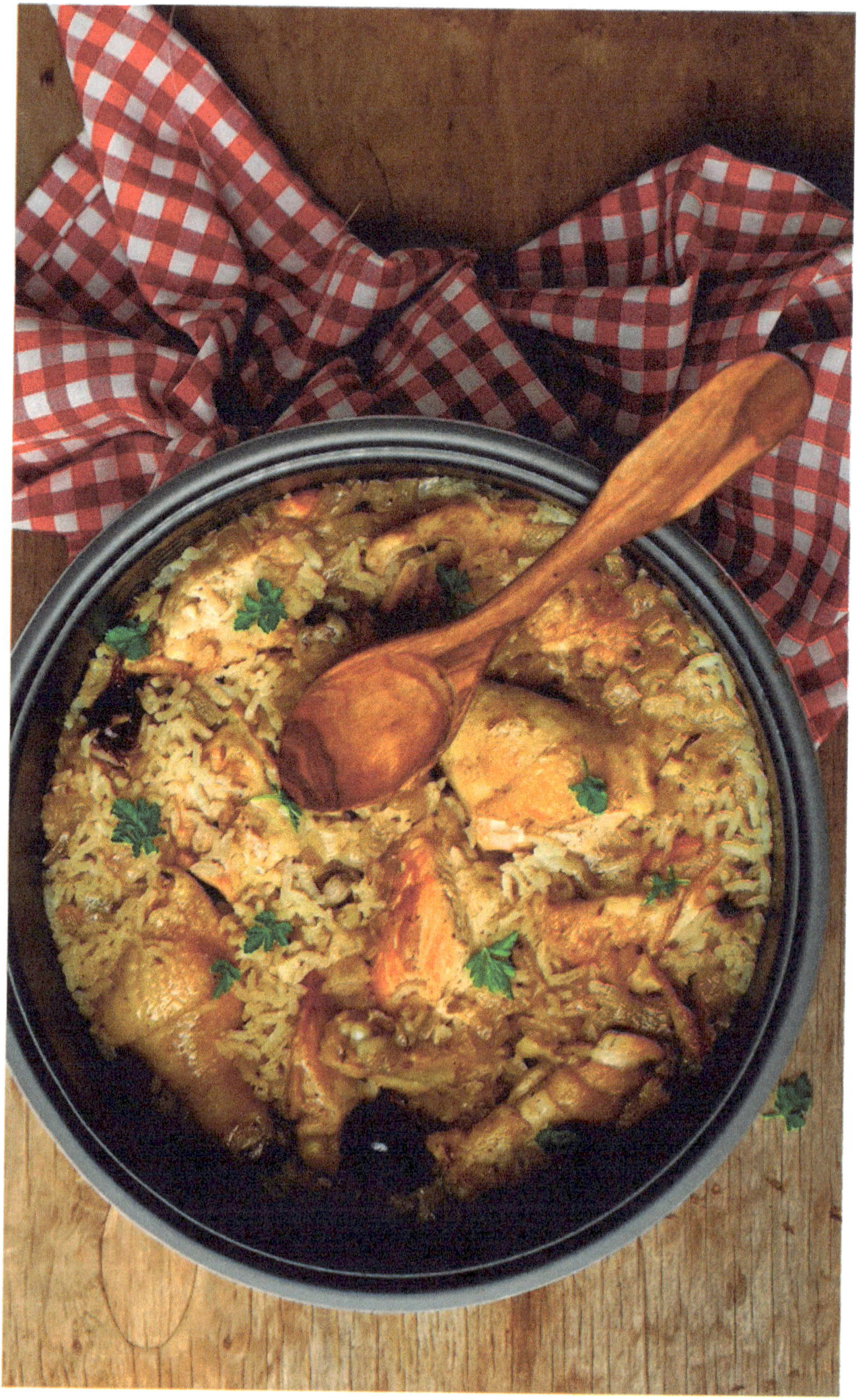

Recipe 18: Stewed Chicken With Rice and Dates

Experience the delightful combination of flavors in Stewed Chicken with Rice and Dates, a Crock Pot dish that infuses the tender chicken with the sweet richness of dates and the comforting texture of rice. It's a unique, easy-to-make meal that's sure to impress.

Servings: 6

Prepping Time: 20 minutes

Cook Time: 5 hours

Difficulty: Medium

Ingredients:

- 4 boneless, skinless chicken breasts
- 1 cup basmati rice
- 1 cup pitted dates, chopped
- 1 large onion, chopped
- 2 cloves garlic, minced
- 2 cups chicken broth
- 1 tsp ground cinnamon
- Salt and pepper to taste

Step-by-Step Preparation:

1. Layer the bottom of the Crock Pot with onion and garlic.
2. Place chicken on top and season with salt, pepper, and cinnamon.
3. Add chopped dates and rice.
4. Pour in chicken broth.
5. Cook on low for 5 hours until chicken and rice are tender.

Nutritional Facts: (Per serving)

- Calories: 310
- Protein: 28g
- Carbohydrates: 40g
- Fat: 4g
- Sodium: 300mg

Stewed Chicken with Rice and Dates is a delightful fusion of savory and sweet, bringing a touch of exotic flair to your dinner table with the ease of Crock Pot cooking.

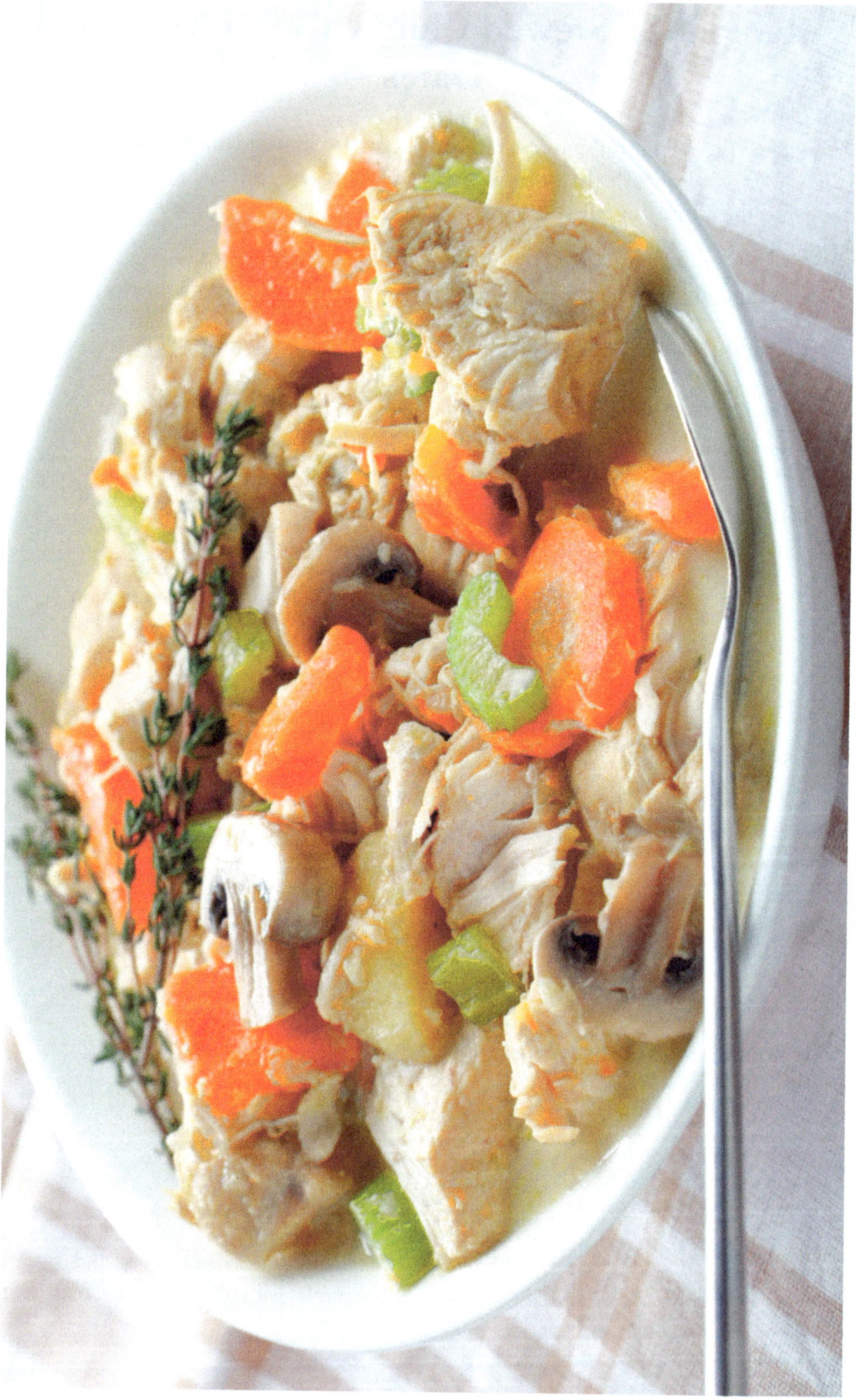

Recipe 19: Chicken Stew With Vegetables

Indulge in the rich and hearty flavors of this Chicken Stew with Vegetables, Mushrooms, Herbs, and Creamy Sauce. Cooked to perfection in a Crock Pot, this dish offers a comforting blend of tender chicken and fresh vegetables enveloped in a luscious, herb-infused sauce.

Servings: 6

Prepping Time: 20 minutes

Cook Time: 6 hours

Difficulty: Medium

Ingredients:
- 4 boneless, skinless chicken breasts
- 2 cups mixed vegetables (carrots, peas, corn)
- 1 cup sliced mushrooms
- 1 onion, chopped
- 2 garlic cloves, minced
- 2 cups chicken broth
- 1 cup heavy cream
- 1 tsp dried thyme
- 1 tsp dried rosemary
- Salt and pepper to taste

Step-by-Step Preparation:
1. Place chicken in the Crock Pot.
2. Add mixed vegetables, mushrooms, onion, and garlic.
3. Pour in chicken broth and sprinkle with thyme, rosemary, salt, and pepper.
4. Cook on low for 6 hours.
5. Stir in heavy cream during the last 30 minutes of cooking.

Nutritional Facts: (Per serving)
- Calories: 320
- Protein: 28g
- Carbohydrates: 12g
- Fat: 18g
- Sodium: 410mg

This Chicken Stew with Vegetables and Creamy Sauce is the epitome of comfort food, combining wholesome ingredients and robust flavors to create a satisfying meal perfect for any occasion.

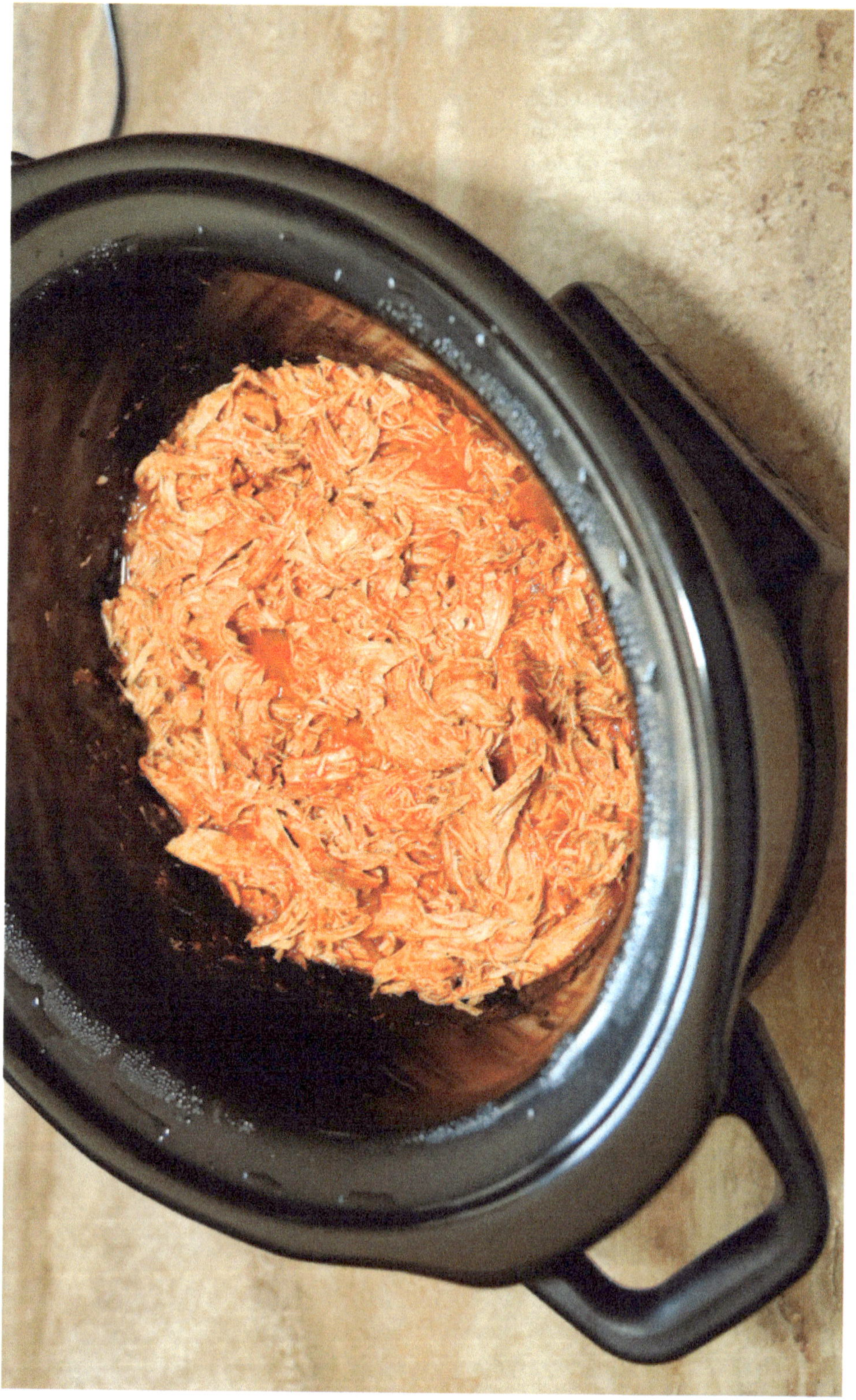

Recipe 20: Chicken Tinga

Chicken Tinga, a versatile and flavorful dish, is perfect for creating delicious tacos, tostadas, soups, or quesadillas. Made in a Crock Pot, this recipe simplifies preparing authentic shredded chicken tinga infused with rich and spicy flavors.

Servings: 8

Prepping Time: 15 minutes

Cook Time: 4 hours

Difficulty: Easy

Ingredients:

- ✓ 4 boneless, skinless chicken breasts
- ✓ 1 can (14 oz) diced tomatoes
- ✓ 1 medium onion, sliced
- ✓ 2 chipotle peppers in adobo sauce, chopped
- ✓ 3 garlic cloves, minced
- ✓ 1 tsp ground cumin
- ✓ Salt and pepper to taste

Step-by-Step Preparation:

1. Place chicken breasts in the Crock Pot.
2. Add diced tomatoes, onion, chipotle peppers, garlic, and cumin.
3. Season with salt and pepper.
4. Cook on low for 4 hours until chicken is tender.
5. Shred the chicken with forks and mix well with the sauce.

Nutritional Facts: (Per serving)

- ❖ Calories: 130
- ❖ Protein: 20g
- ❖ Carbohydrates: 4g
- ❖ Fat: 3g
- ❖ Sodium: 320mg

Enjoy the ease and delightful taste of Chicken Tinga, perfect for a Mexican-inspired meal. Whether wrapped in a taco, layered on a tostada, or stuffed in a quesadilla, it's guaranteed to be a hit!

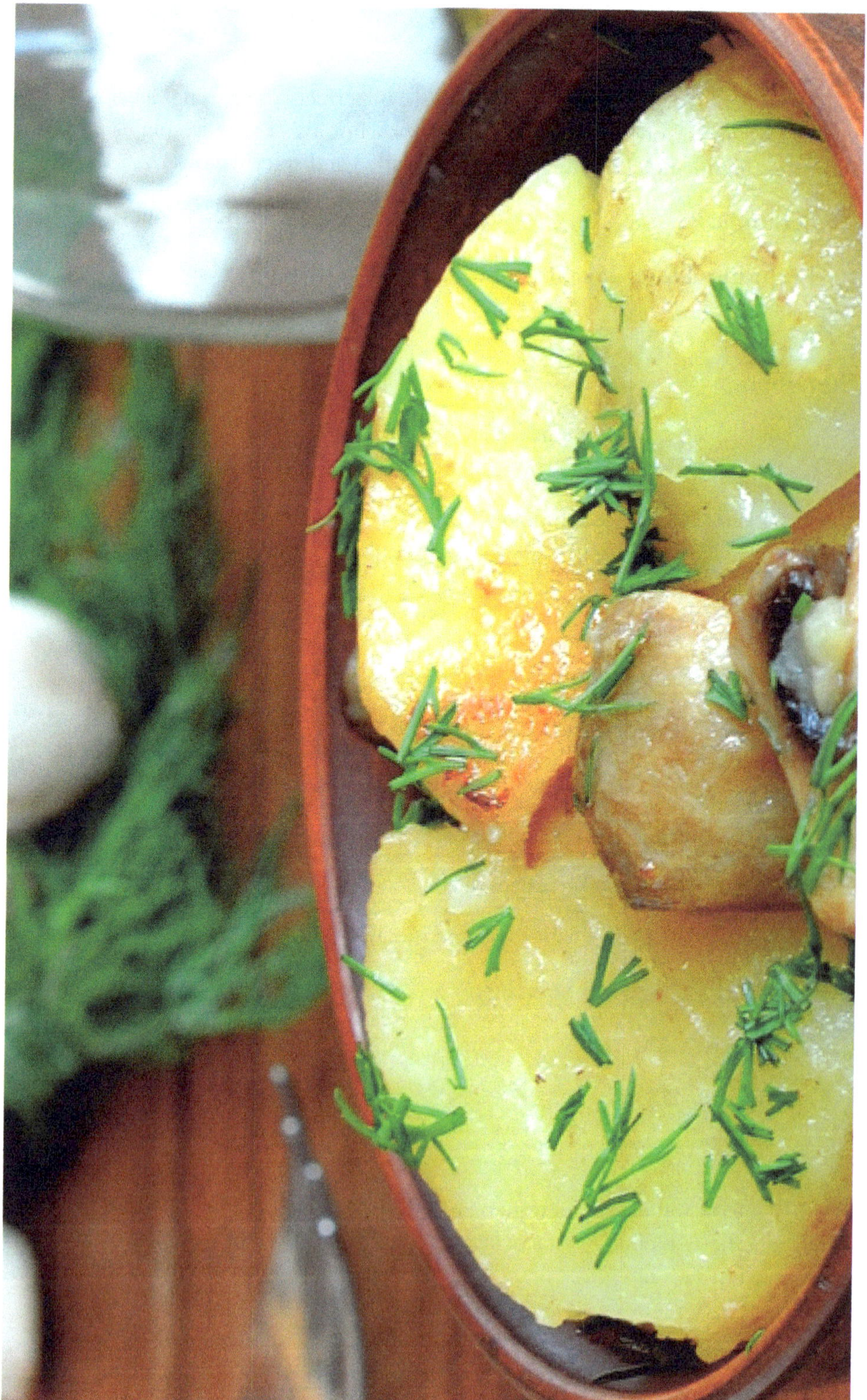

Chapter 03: Verdant Veggie Varieties

Recipe 21: Mushroom and Potato Stew

Discover the heartwarming flavors of Vegetarian Mushroom and Potato Stew, a Crock Pot recipe that combines earthy mushrooms and hearty potatoes seasoned with fresh dill and a hint of salt. It's a comforting, easy-to-make dish perfect for vegetarians and anyone looking for a satisfying meat-free meal.

Servings: 6

Prepping Time: 15 minutes

Cook Time: 5 hours

Difficulty: Easy

Ingredients:

- 2 cups sliced mushrooms
- 4 large potatoes, cubed
- 1 onion, chopped
- 3 cloves garlic, minced
- 4 cups vegetable broth
- 1 tbsp fresh dill, chopped
- Salt and pepper to taste

Step-by-Step Preparation:

1. Add mushrooms, potatoes, onion, and garlic to the Crock Pot.
2. Pour in vegetable broth.
3. Season with salt, pepper, and fresh dill.
4. Cook on low for 5 hours until vegetables are tender.
5. Adjust seasoning as needed before serving.

Nutritional Facts: (Per serving)

- Calories: 150
- Protein: 4g
- Carbohydrates: 33g
- Fat: 0.5g
- Sodium: 500mg

Enjoy the simple yet delicious Vegetarian Mushroom and Potato Stew, a dish that brings the essence of home cooking to your table, offering warmth and nourishment in every spoonful.

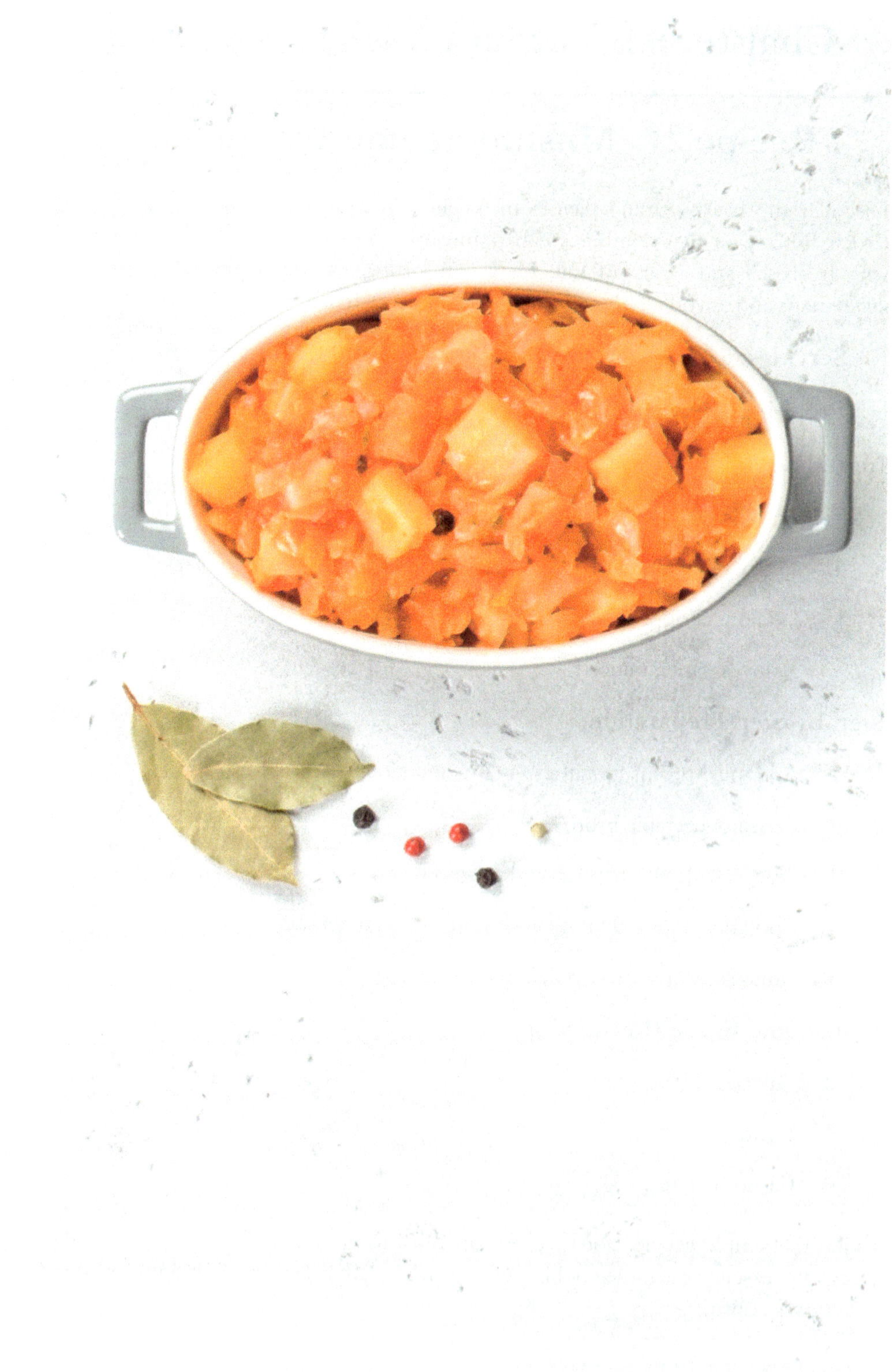

Recipe 22: Stewed Cabbage Potato

Stewed Cabbage Potato, a simple yet hearty Crock Pot vegetarian dish, combines the comforting flavors of cabbage and potatoes. This easy-to-make recipe is perfect for those seeking a wholesome, nutritious meal that's both satisfying and flavorful.

Servings: 6

Cook Time: 6 hours

Prepping Time: 15 minutes

Difficulty: Easy

Ingredients:

- 1 medium head of cabbage, chopped
- 4 large potatoes, cubed
- 1 onion, chopped
- 2 cloves garlic, minced
- 3 cups vegetable broth
- 1 tsp paprika
- Salt and pepper to taste

Step-by-Step Preparation:

1. Place cabbage, potatoes, onion, and garlic in the Crock Pot.
2. Pour vegetable broth over the vegetables.
3. Season with paprika, salt, and pepper.
4. Cook on low for 6 hours until vegetables are tender.
5. Stir well before serving.

Nutritional Facts: (Per serving)

- Calories: 120
- Protein: 3g
- Carbohydrates: 27g
- Fat: 0.5g
- Sodium: 480mg

Enjoy the simplicity and comfort of Stewed Cabbage Potato, a dish that embodies the essence of home-cooked meals, providing a warm and nourishing experience with every bite.

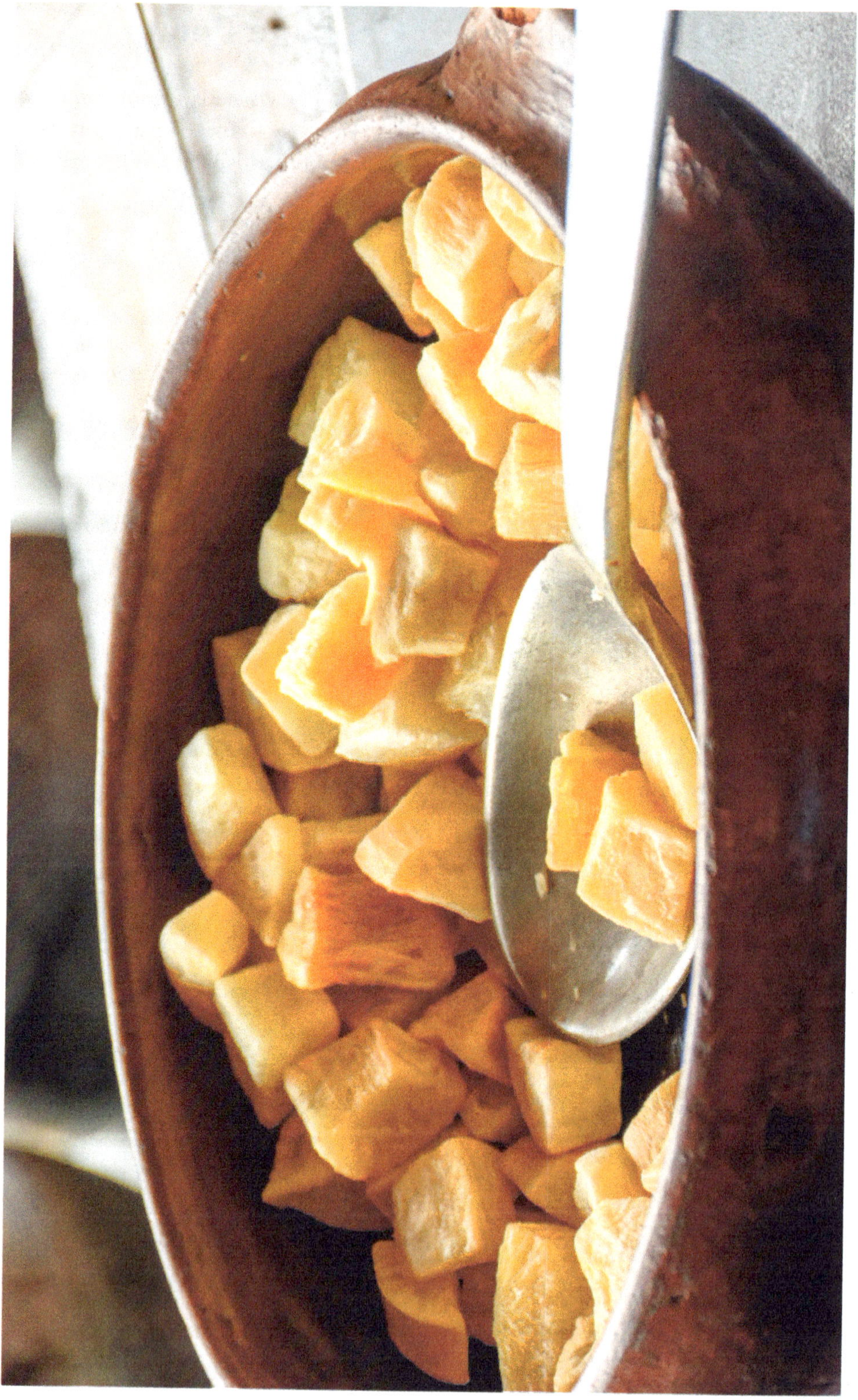

Recipe 23: Fried Cassava

Fried Cassava, a delightful Crock Pot dish, transforms the humble Cassava into a crispy, golden treat. This vegetarian recipe is perfect for those who enjoy exploring different cuisines and textures in their cooking, offering a unique and tasty experience.

Servings: 4

Prepping Time: 10 minutes

Cook Time: 3 hours

Difficulty: Medium

Ingredients:

- ✓ 4 cups cassava, peeled and sliced
- ✓ 3 tbsp olive oil
- ✓ 2 cloves garlic, minced
- ✓ Salt to taste
- ✓ Optional: herbs or spices for seasoning

Step-by-Step Preparation:

1. Toss cassava slices with olive oil, garlic, and salt in a bowl.
2. Place in the Crock Pot in a single layer.
3. Cook on high for 3 hours or until Cassava is golden and crispy.
4. Optionally, sprinkle with your favorite herbs or spices before serving.

Nutritional Facts: (Per serving)

- ❖ Calories: 220
- ❖ Protein: 2g
- ❖ Carbohydrates: 40g
- ❖ Fat: 7g
- ❖ Sodium: 10mg

Enjoy the unique and satisfying taste of Fried Cassava, a simple yet exotic dish that brings a crunchy and flavorful twist to your vegetarian meals.

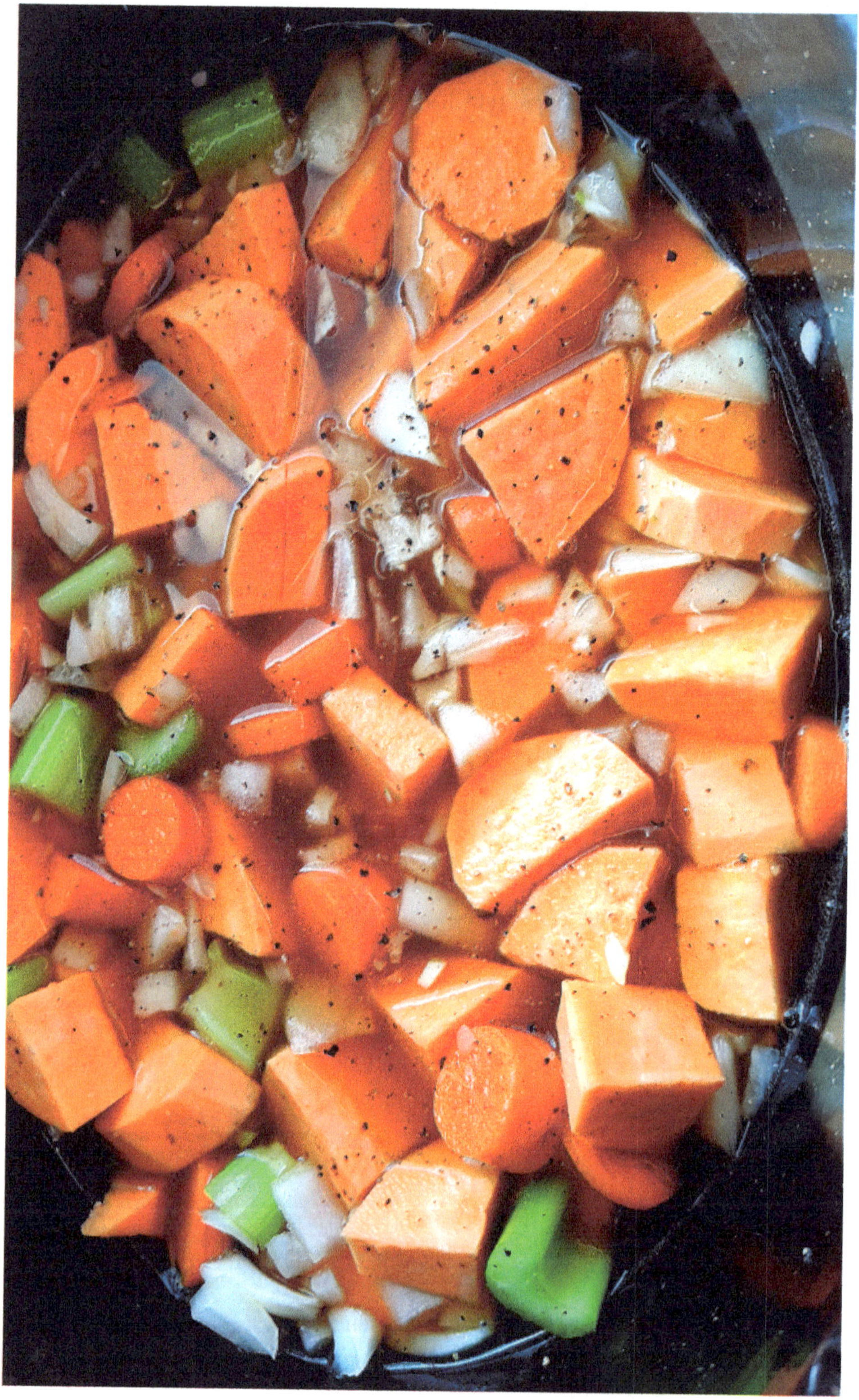

Recipe 24: Carrot and Celery Stew

Carrot and Celery Stew is a nourishing Crock Pot vegetarian dish, combining the subtle sweetness of carrots with the crisp freshness of celery. This easy-to-prepare stew is perfect for a healthy, comforting meal and is ideal for those seeking flavor and simplicity in their cooking.

Servings: 6

Prepping Time: 15 minutes

Cook Time: 6 hours

Difficulty: Easy

Ingredients:

- 4 large carrots, sliced
- 4 celery stalks, chopped
- 1 onion, diced
- 2 garlic cloves, minced
- 3 cups vegetable broth
- 1 tsp dried thyme
- Salt and pepper to taste

Step-by-Step Preparation:

1. Add carrots, celery, onion, and garlic to the Crock Pot.
2. Pour in vegetable broth.
3. Season with thyme, salt, and pepper.
4. Cook on low for 6 hours until vegetables are tender.
5. Adjust seasoning as needed before serving.

Nutritional Facts: (Per serving)

- Calories: 50
- Protein: 1g
- Carbohydrates: 11g
- Fat: 0g
- Sodium: 500mg

Enjoy the simple yet delightful flavors of Carrot and Celery Stew, a dish that offers a comforting embrace in every spoonful, perfect for cozy nights or healthy, wholesome meals.

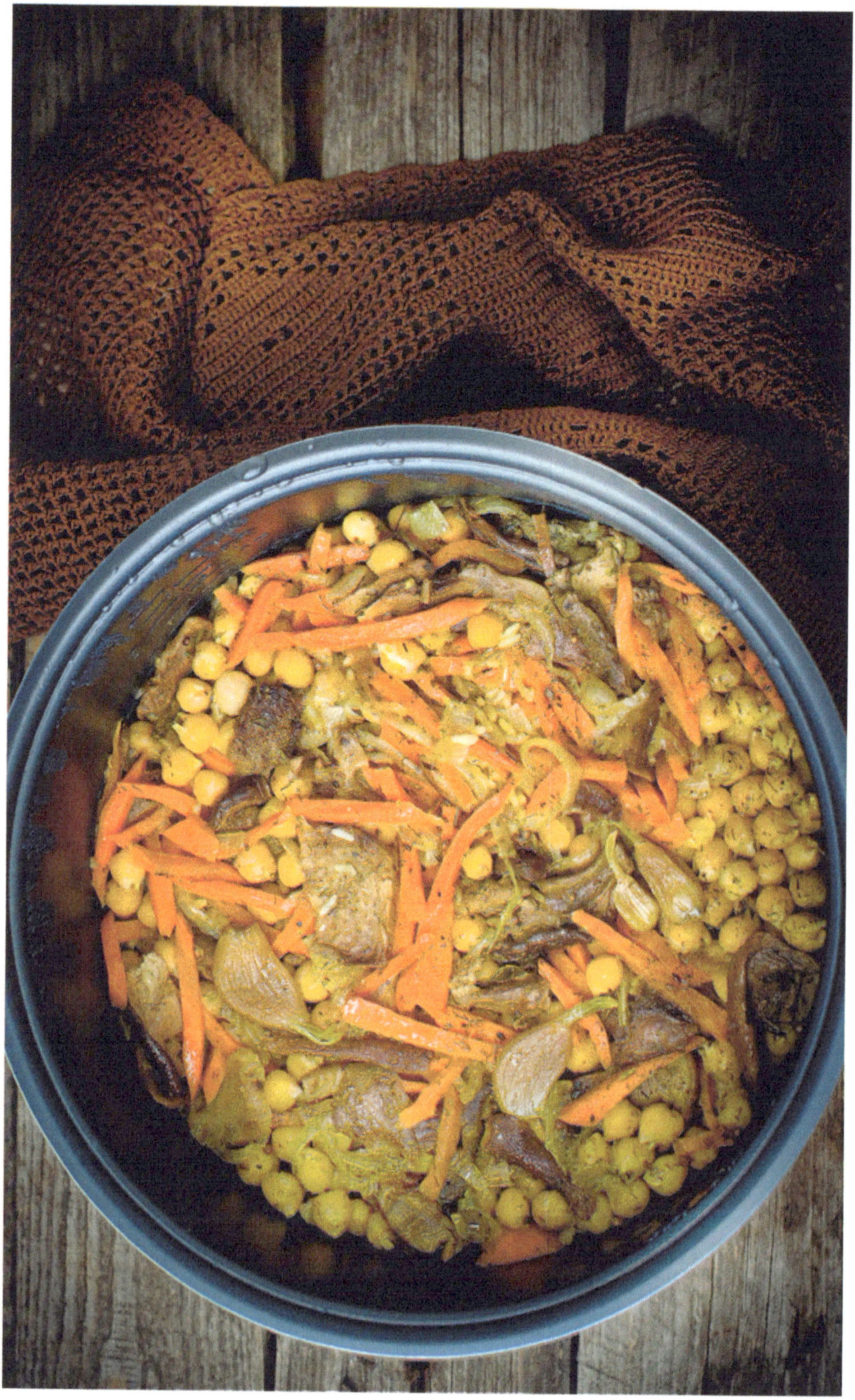

Recipe 25: Pilaf With Chick-Pea and Mushrooms

Pilaf with Chick-Pak Chickpeas and Mushrooms brings a delightful combination of flavors and textures to your table. This Crock Pot vegetarian recipe is easy to prepare and offers a healthy and satisfying meal, perfect for anyone looking to enjoy a delicious blend of grains and vegetables.

Servings: 6

Prepping Time: 20 minutes

Cook Time: 4 hours

Difficulty: Medium

Ingredients:

- 1 cup basmati rice
- 1 can chickpeas, drained and rinsed
- 2 cups sliced mushrooms
- 1 onion, chopped
- 2 cloves garlic, minced
- 2 1/2 cups vegetable broth
- 1 tsp cumin
- Salt and pepper to taste

Step-by-Step Preparation:

1. Rinse basmati rice and place it in the Crock Pot.
2. Add chickpeas, mushrooms, onion, and garlic.
3. Pour in vegetable broth and season with cumin, salt, and pepper.
4. Stir gently to combine.
5. Cook on low for 4 hours, until rice is tender and fluffy.

Nutritional Facts: (Per serving)

- Calories: 210
- Protein: 7g
- Carbohydrates: 40g
- Fat: 2g
- Sodium: 400mg

Enjoy Pilaf with Chickpeas and Mushrooms, a dish that's nourishing and full of flavor, making it an ideal choice for a wholesome and hearty vegetarian meal.

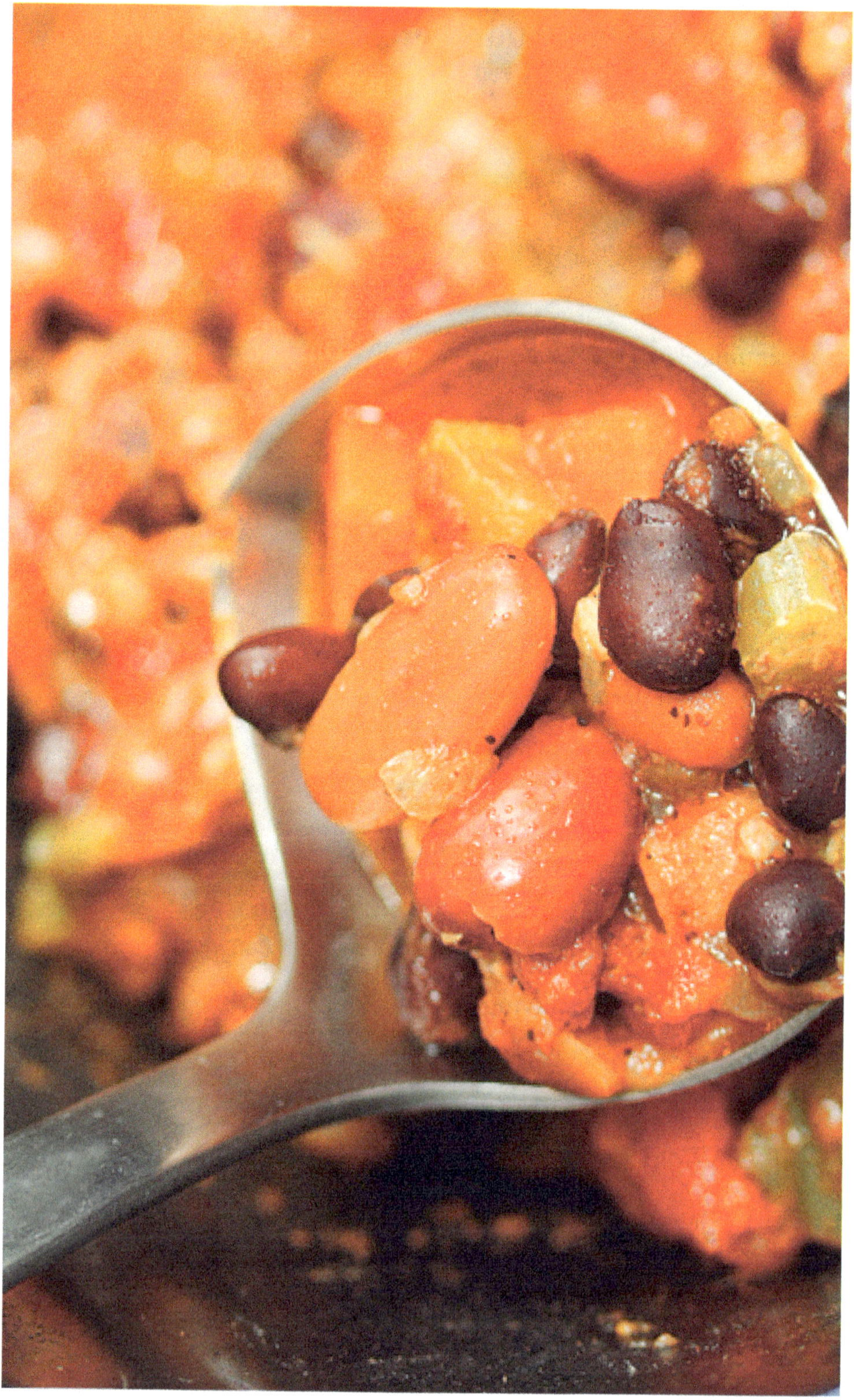

Recipe 26: Vegetarian Crock Pot Chili

Vegetarian Crock Pot Chili offers a hearty and flavorsome meal that's satisfying and simple to prepare. Perfect for those seeking a comforting, meat-free option, this chili is packed with rich spices and various vegetables, making it a favorite for any time of the year.

Servings: 8

Prepping Time: 15 minutes

Cook Time: 6-8 hours

Difficulty: Easy

Ingredients:

- 2 cans kidney beans, drained and rinsed
- 1 can black beans, drained and rinsed
- 2 cans diced tomatoes
- 1 onion, chopped
- 1 bell pepper, chopped
- 2 cloves garlic, minced
- 2 tbsp chili powder
- 1 tsp cumin
- 1 tsp paprika
- Salt and pepper to taste

Step-by-Step Preparation:

1. Add all beans, tomatoes, onion, bell pepper, and garlic to the Crock Pot.
2. Season with chili powder, cumin, paprika, salt, and pepper.
3. Stir to combine all ingredients well.
4. Cook on low for 6-8 hours, allowing flavors to meld.
5. Adjust seasoning if necessary before serving.

Nutritional Facts: (Per serving)

- Calories: 200
- Protein: 12g
- Carbohydrates: 35g
- Fat: 1g
- Sodium: 300mg

This Vegetarian Crock Pot Chili is not just a dish; it's a warm, inviting bowl of comfort, perfect for cozy nights or feeding a crowd with a nutritious, delicious meal.

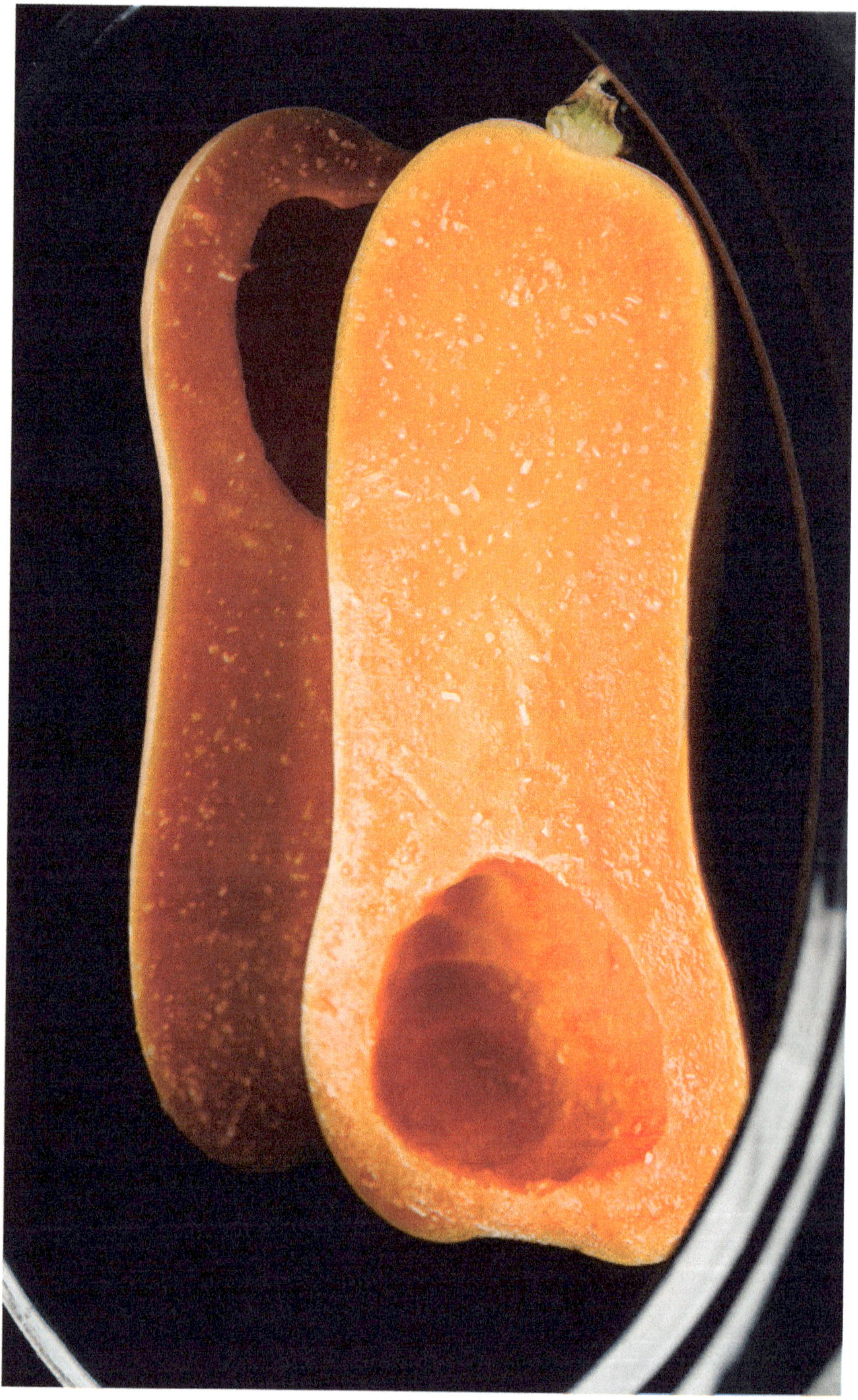

Recipe 27: Halves of a Butternut Squash

"Two Halves of a Butternut Squash" is a delightfully simple yet flavorful Crock Pot vegetarian recipe. This dish highlights butternut squash's natural sweetness and soft texture, making it an excellent choice for a healthy, fuss-free meal or a comforting side dish.

Servings: 2

Prepping Time: 5 minutes

Cook Time: 3-4 hours

Difficulty: Easy

Ingredients:

- 1 large butternut squash, halved and seeds removed
- 2 tbsp maple syrup
- 1 tbsp olive oil
- Salt and pepper to taste
- Optional: a pinch of cinnamon or nutmeg

Step-by-Step Preparation:

1. Brush each half of the squash with olive oil and maple syrup.
2. Season with salt, pepper, and optional spices.
3. Place the squash halves in the Crock Pot and cut side up.
4. Cook on low for 3-4 hours until tender.
5. Serve warm as a delicious and nutritious dish.

Nutritional Facts: (Per serving)

- Calories: 180
- Protein: 2g
- Carbohydrates: 40g
- Fat: 5g
- Sodium: 20mg

Savor the effortless charm of "Two Halves of a Butternut Squash," a recipe that offers a perfect balance of sweetness and warmth, ideal for cozy nights or as a nutritious addition to any meal.

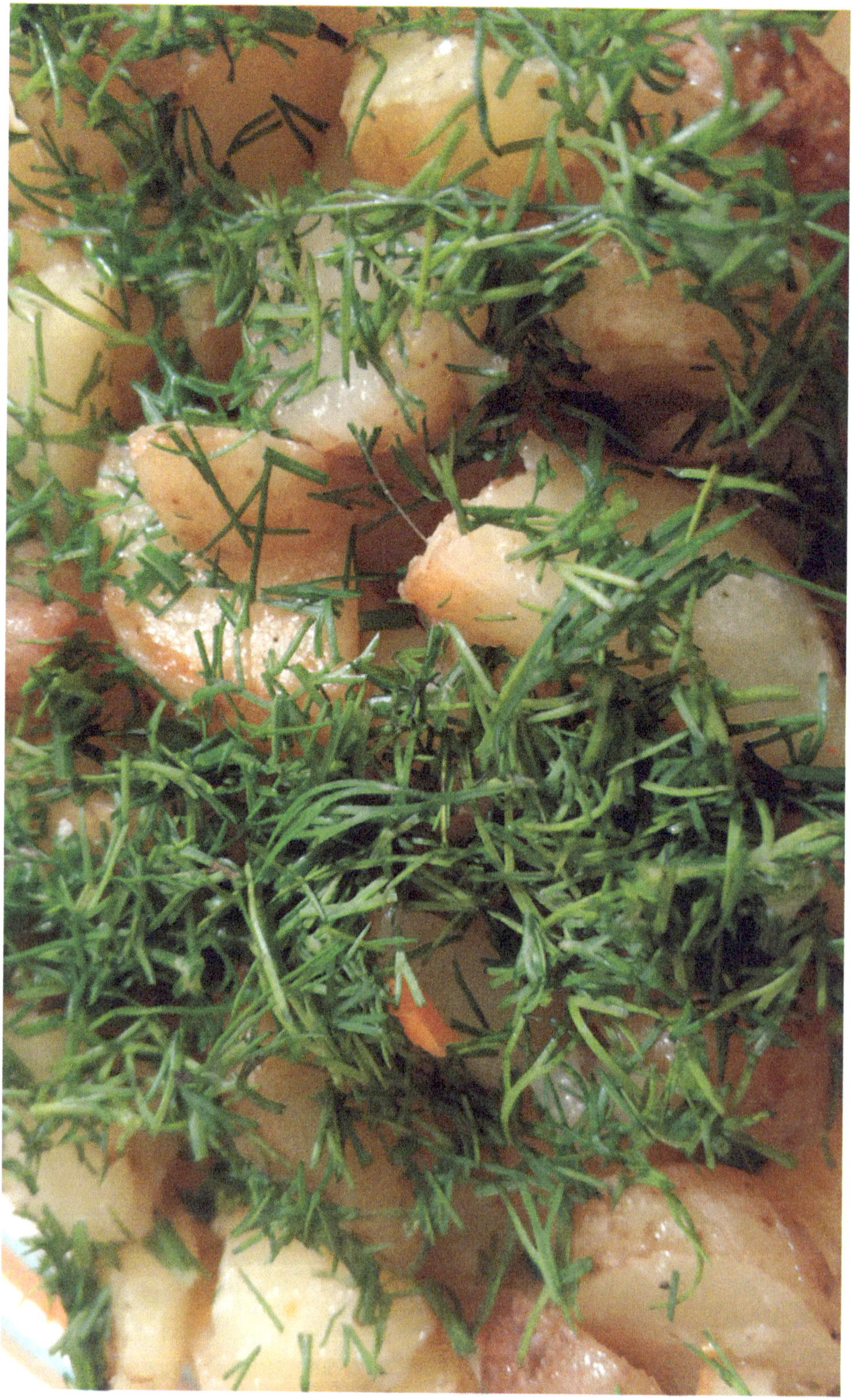

Recipe 28: Young Potatoes Sprinkled With Dill

"Young Potatoes Sprinkled with Dill" is a simple yet delicious Crock Pot vegetarian recipe. It pairs young potatoes' tender, earthy flavors with the fresh, aromatic taste of dill. This dish is ideal for anyone seeking a comforting and easy-to-prepare side or main course.

Servings: 4

Prepping Time: 10 minutes

Cook Time: 4 hours

Difficulty: Easy

Ingredients:

- 2 lbs young potatoes, scrubbed and halved
- 2 tbsp olive oil
- 3 tbsp fresh dill, chopped
- Salt and pepper to taste

Step-by-Step Preparation:

1. Toss potatoes with olive oil, salt, and pepper in a bowl.
2. Place potatoes in the Crock Pot.
3. Cook on low for 4 hours until tender.
4. Sprinkle with fresh dill before serving.

Nutritional Facts: (Per serving)

- Calories: 160
- Protein: 4g
- Carbohydrates: 28g
- Fat: 4g
- Sodium: 10mg

Enjoy the wholesome goodness of "Young Potatoes Sprinkled with Dill," a delightful dish that brings comfort and flavor to your table with minimal effort, making it a perfect choice for busy days or relaxed gatherings.

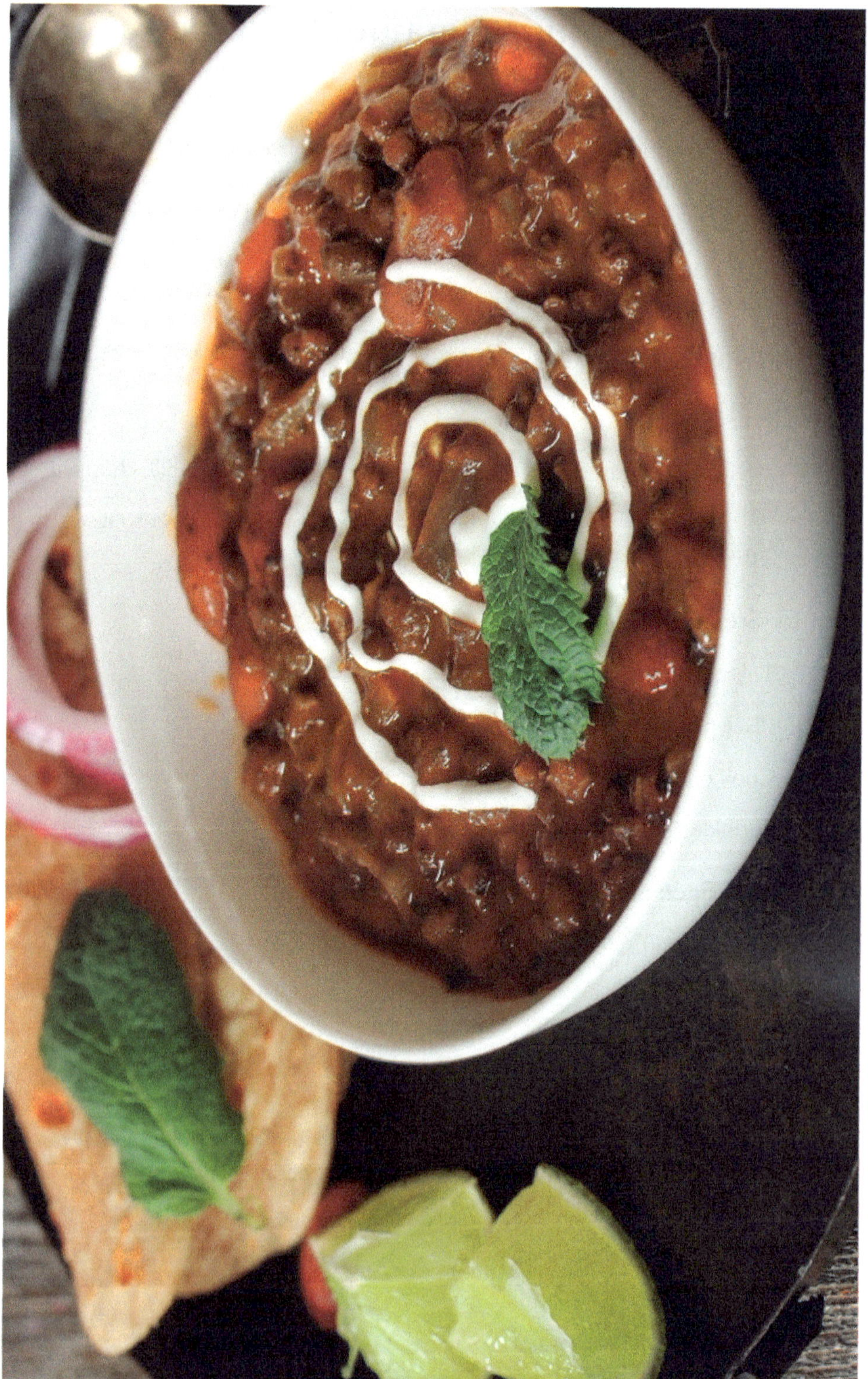

Recipe 29: Curry With Black Lentils and Red Kidney Beans

Dal Makhani is a rich and flavorsome Indian curry, a staple in many households. This Crock Pot version combines black lentils and red kidney beans, simmered to perfection and typically served with Roti or Paratha. It's an ideal recipe for anyone looking to enjoy a classic, heartwarming vegetarian dish.

Servings: 6

Prepping Time: 10 minutes (plus overnight soaking)

Cook Time: 8 hours

Difficulty: Medium

Ingredients:

- 1 cup black lentils (urad dal), soaked overnight
- 1/2 cup red kidney beans, soaked overnight
- 1 onion, finely chopped
- 2 tomatoes, pureed
- 3 garlic cloves, minced
- 1 inch ginger, minced
- 2 tbsp butter
- 1 cup cream
- 1 tsp cumin seeds
- 1 tsp garam masala
- Salt to taste

Step-by-Step Preparation:

1. Drain and rinse lentils and kidney beans. Place in the Crock Pot.
2. Add chopped onion, tomato puree, garlic, and ginger.
3. Pour enough water to cover the mixture.
4. Cook on low for 8 hours until lentils and beans are tender.
5. Stir in butter, cream, cumin seeds, garam masala, and salt.
6. Cook for another 30 minutes.

Nutritional Facts: (Per serving)

- Calories: 350
- Protein: 18g
- Carbohydrates: 40g
- Fat: 15g
- Sodium: 200mg

Dal Makhani in a Crock Pot offers a delightful combination of taste and comfort, perfect for a nourishing meal any day of the week. It's a testament to the rich culinary heritage of Indian cuisine brought to life in your kitchen.

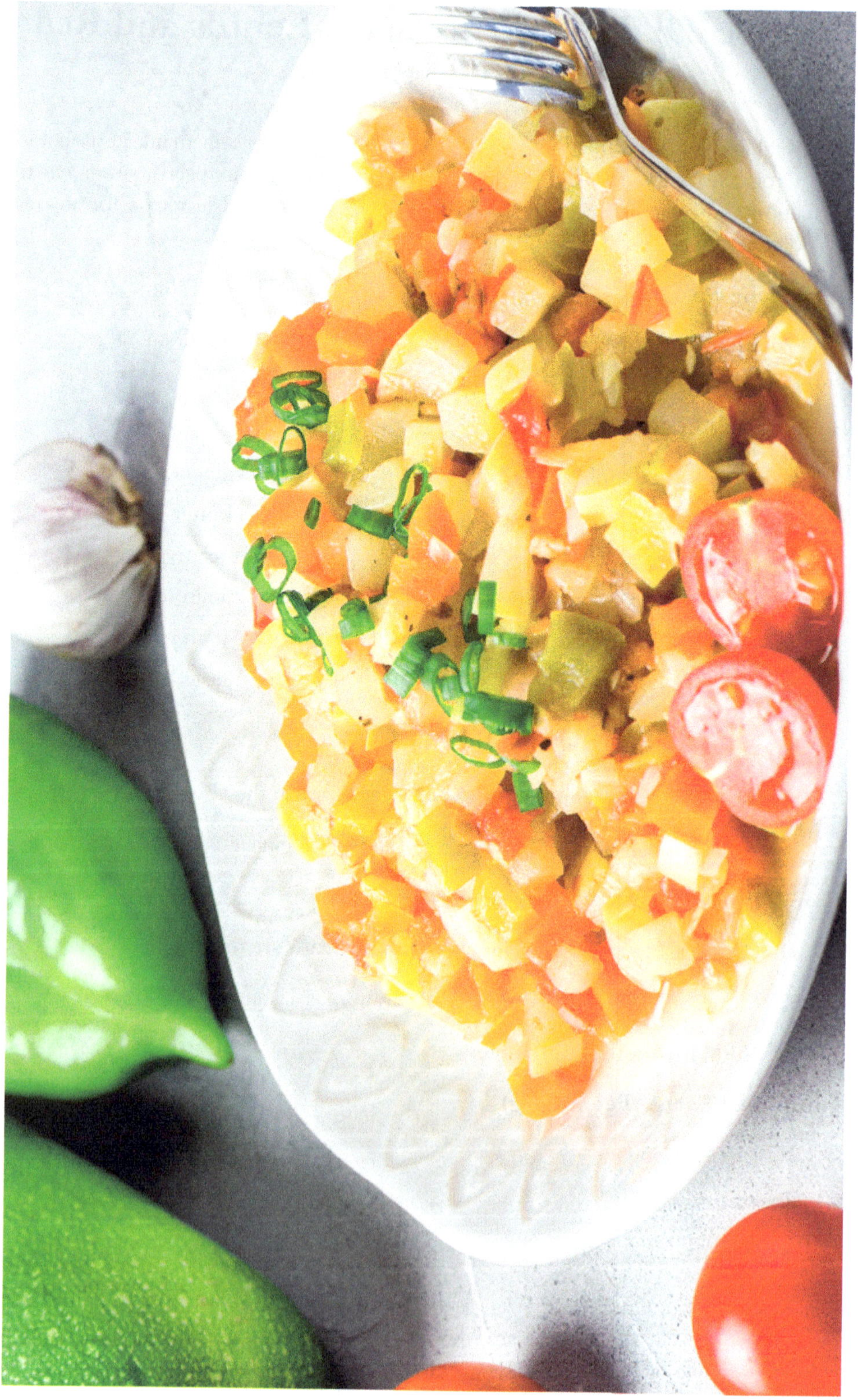

Recipe 30: Zucchini, Tomatoes, Bell Pepper and Garlic Stew

Zucchini, Tomatoes, Bell Pepper, and Garlic Stew is a vibrant and flavorful Crock Pot vegetarian dish. Packed with fresh vegetables and seasoned to perfection, this stew is both healthy and satisfying, ideal for those seeking a delicious, easy-to-make meal filled with the goodness of garden-fresh produce.

Servings: 6

Prepping Time: 15 minutes

Cook Time: 6 hours

Difficulty: Easy

Ingredients:

- 3 medium zucchinis, sliced
- 2 large tomatoes, chopped
- 1 bell pepper, chopped
- 4 cloves garlic, minced
- 1 onion, chopped
- 2 cups vegetable broth
- 1 tsp dried basil
- 1 tsp dried oregano
- Salt and pepper to taste

Step-by-Step Preparation:

1. Place zucchini, tomatoes, bell pepper, garlic, and onion in the Crock Pot.
2. Add vegetable broth and sprinkle with basil, oregano, salt, and pepper.
3. Stir gently to mix the ingredients.
4. Cook on low for 6 hours until vegetables are tender.
5. Adjust seasoning if necessary before serving.

Nutritional Facts: (Per serving)

- Calories: 60
- Protein: 2g
- Carbohydrates: 13g
- Fat: 0.5g
- Sodium: 320mg

Enjoy the delightful blend of flavors in this Zucchini, Tomatoes, Bell Pepper, and Garlic Stew. This dish is as nourishing as it is delicious, perfect for a wholesome and comforting meal any time.

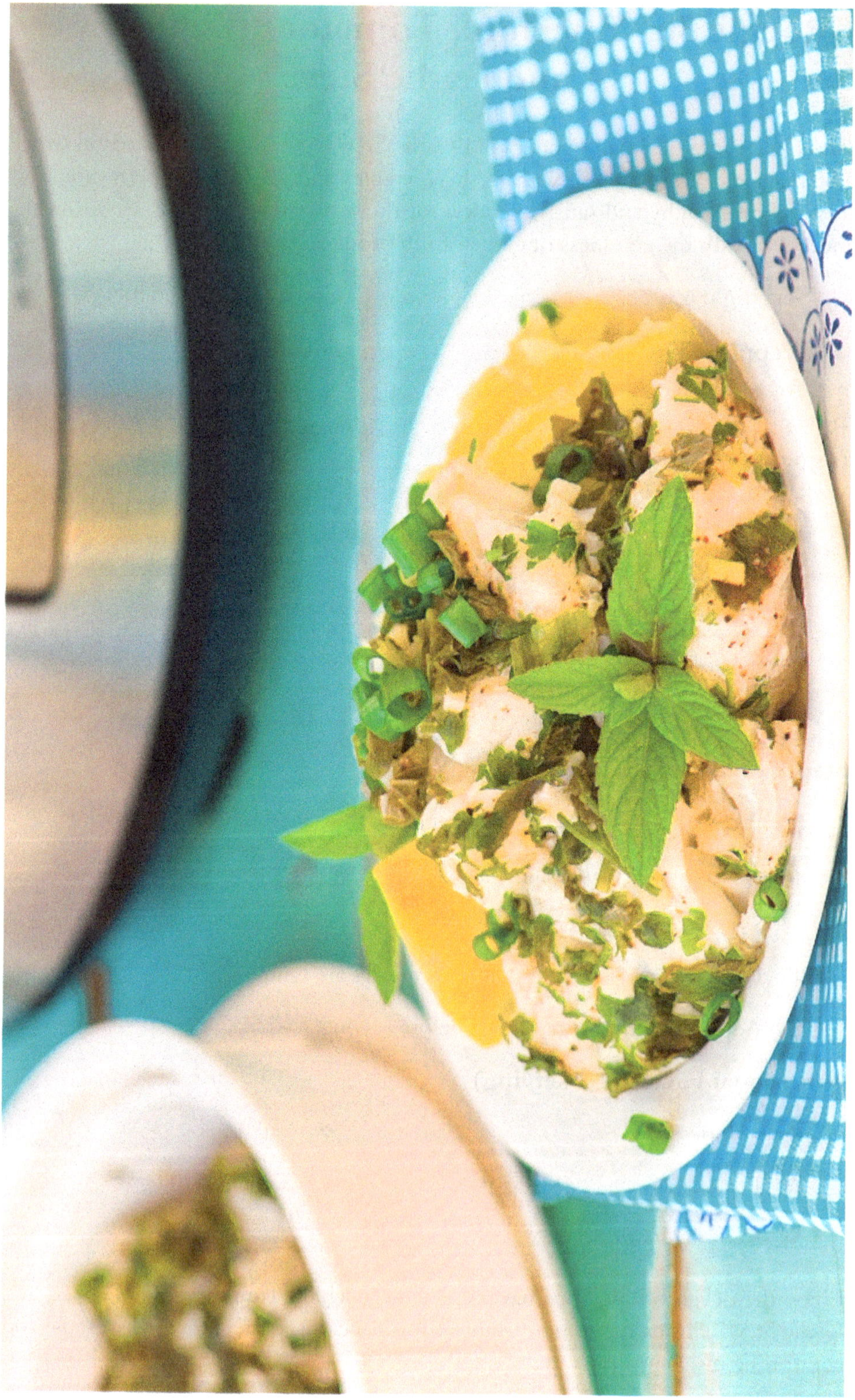

Chapter 04: Ocean-Inspired Eats

Recipe 31: Cod Fillet With Greens Steamed

Immerse yourself in the light and healthy flavors of Cod Fillet with steamed greens, a dish that elegantly combines the delicacy of cod with a medley of fresh greens. This Crock Pot recipe is perfect for those who appreciate a nutritious, seafood-focused meal that's effortless to prepare.

Servings: 4

Prepping Time: 10 minutes

Cook Time: 2-3 hours

Difficulty: Easy

Ingredients:

- 4 cod fillets
- 1 cup of mixed greens (spinach, kale, chard)
- 2 cloves garlic, minced
- 1 lemon, sliced
- Salt and pepper to taste
- Optional: herbs like dill or parsley

Step-by-Step Preparation:

1. Arrange cod fillets at the bottom of the Crock Pot.
2. Top with mixed greens and minced garlic.
3. Season with salt and pepper. Place lemon slices over the top.
4. Cook on low for 2-3 hours or until cod is cooked through and flaky.
5. Optionally, garnish with fresh herbs before serving.

Nutritional Facts: (Per serving)

- Calories: 120
- Protein: 20g
- Carbohydrates: 2g
- Fat: 3g
- Sodium: 70mg

This Cod Fillet with Greens Steamed is not just a meal but a celebration of simplicity and health, perfect for a light dinner or a nutritious lunch, bringing together the best of the sea and the garden.

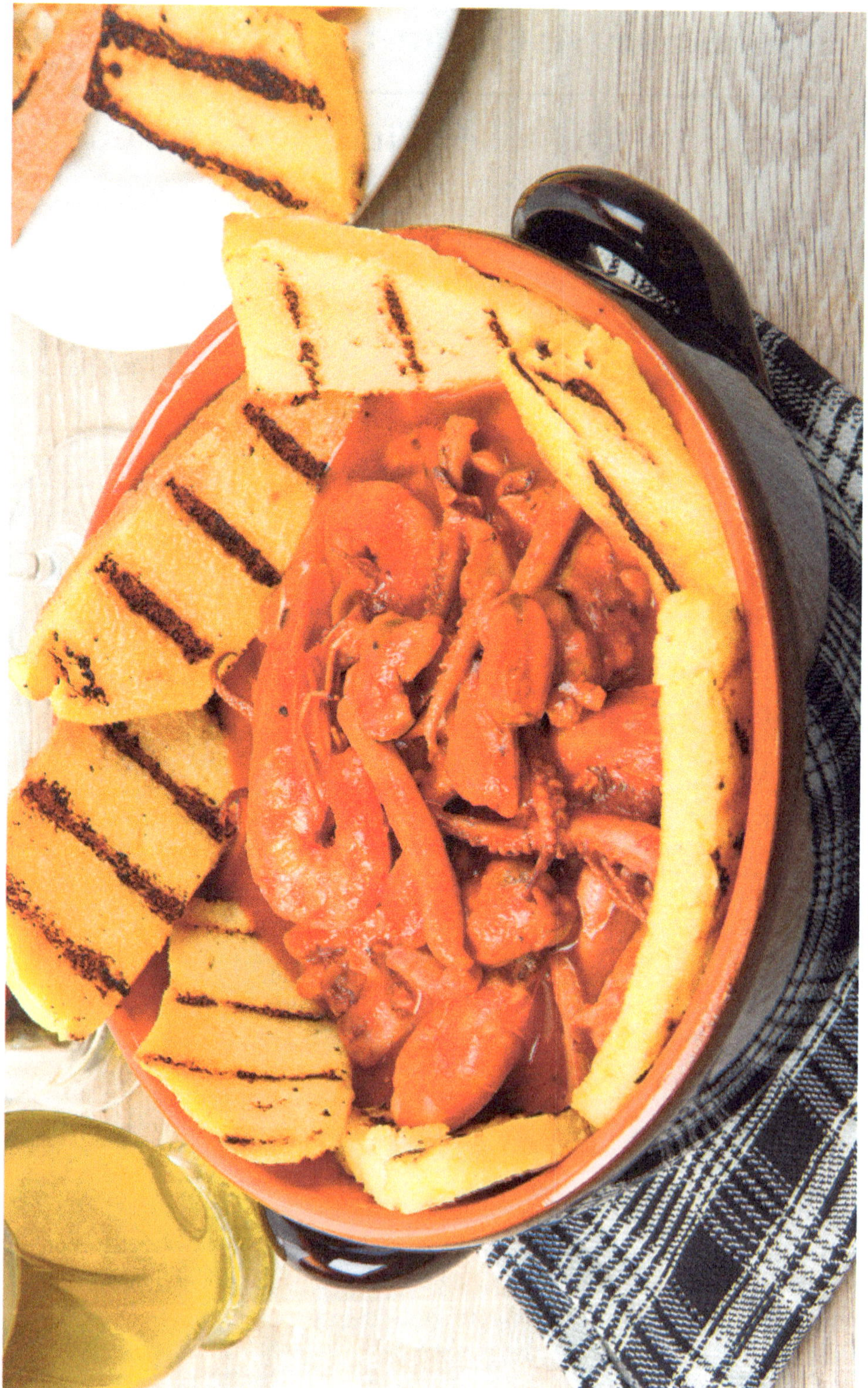

Recipe 32: Fish Soup With Grilled Polenta

Indulge in the savory and comforting flavors of Fish Soup with Grilled Polenta, a delightful combination of a rich, aromatic fish broth with the rustic charm of grilled polenta. This recipe is a nod to traditional cooking, bringing a sophisticated yet easy-to-make dish to your Crock Pot collection.

Servings: 6

Prepping Time: 20 minutes

Cook Time: 4 hours

Difficulty: Medium

Ingredients:

- 4 fish fillets, cubed
- 1 onion, chopped
- 2 carrots, sliced
- 2 celery stalks, chopped
- 4 cups fish broth
- 1 cup polenta
- 2 garlic cloves, minced
- 1 tsp dried thyme
- Salt and pepper to taste

Step-by-Step Preparation:

1. Place fish, onion, carrots, celery, and garlic in the Crock Pot.
2. Pour in fish broth and season with thyme, salt, and pepper.
3. Cook on low for 4 hours.
4. Near the end, grill polenta until crispy and golden.
5. Serve soup hot with a side of grilled polenta.

Nutritional Facts: (Per serving)

- Calories: 220
- Protein: 20g
- Carbohydrates: 23g
- Fat: 4g
- Sodium: 400mg

Fish Soup with Grilled Polenta is more than just a meal; it's a culinary experience that brings together the best of the sea and the earth, making it a perfect dish for those special evenings or a comforting weekend lunch.

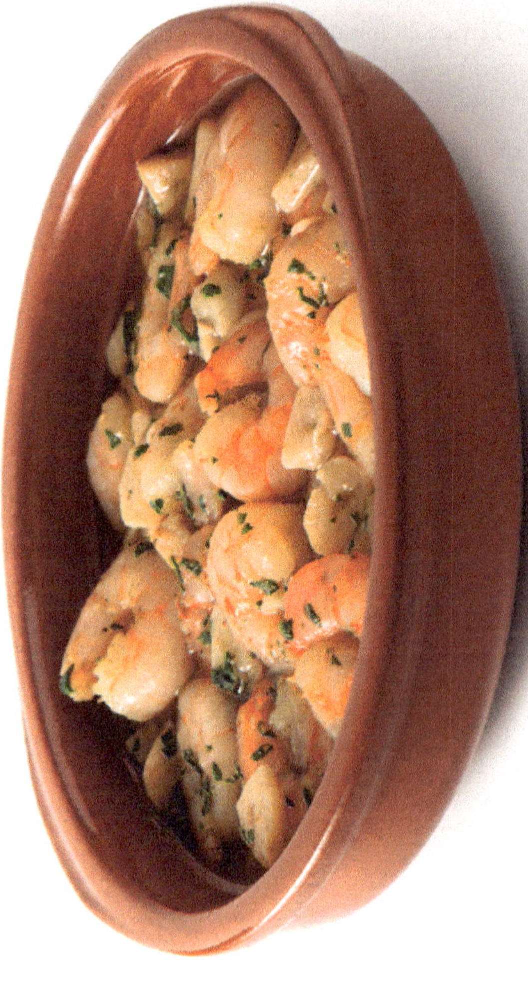

Recipe 33: Garlic Prawns

Garlic Prawns in a Crock Pot offers a compelling blend of succulent prawns and rich garlic flavor, creating a dish that's both simple to prepare and deliciously satisfying. This recipe is perfect for seafood lovers looking for a quick, easy, and flavorful meal that's sure to impress.

Servings: 4

Prepping Time: 15 minutes

Cook Time: 2-3 hours

Difficulty: Easy

Ingredients:

- 2 lbs prawns, peeled and deveined
- 6 cloves garlic, minced
- 1/4 cup olive oil
- 1 lemon, juiced
- 1 tsp paprika
- Salt and pepper to taste
- Fresh parsley, chopped for garnish

Step-by-Step Preparation:

1. Place prawns in the Crock Pot.
2. Mix garlic, olive oil, lemon juice, paprika, salt, and pepper in a bowl.
3. Pour the mixture over the prawns.
4. Cook on low for 2-3 hours until prawns are pink and tender.
5. Garnish with fresh parsley before serving.

Nutritional Facts: (Per serving)

- Calories: 250
- Protein: 35g
- Carbohydrates: 3g
- Fat: 10g
- Sodium: 300mg

Enjoy Garlic Prawns, a dish that combines the ease of Crock Pot cooking with the gourmet taste of a seafood restaurant, perfect for a special occasion or a delightful weeknight treat.

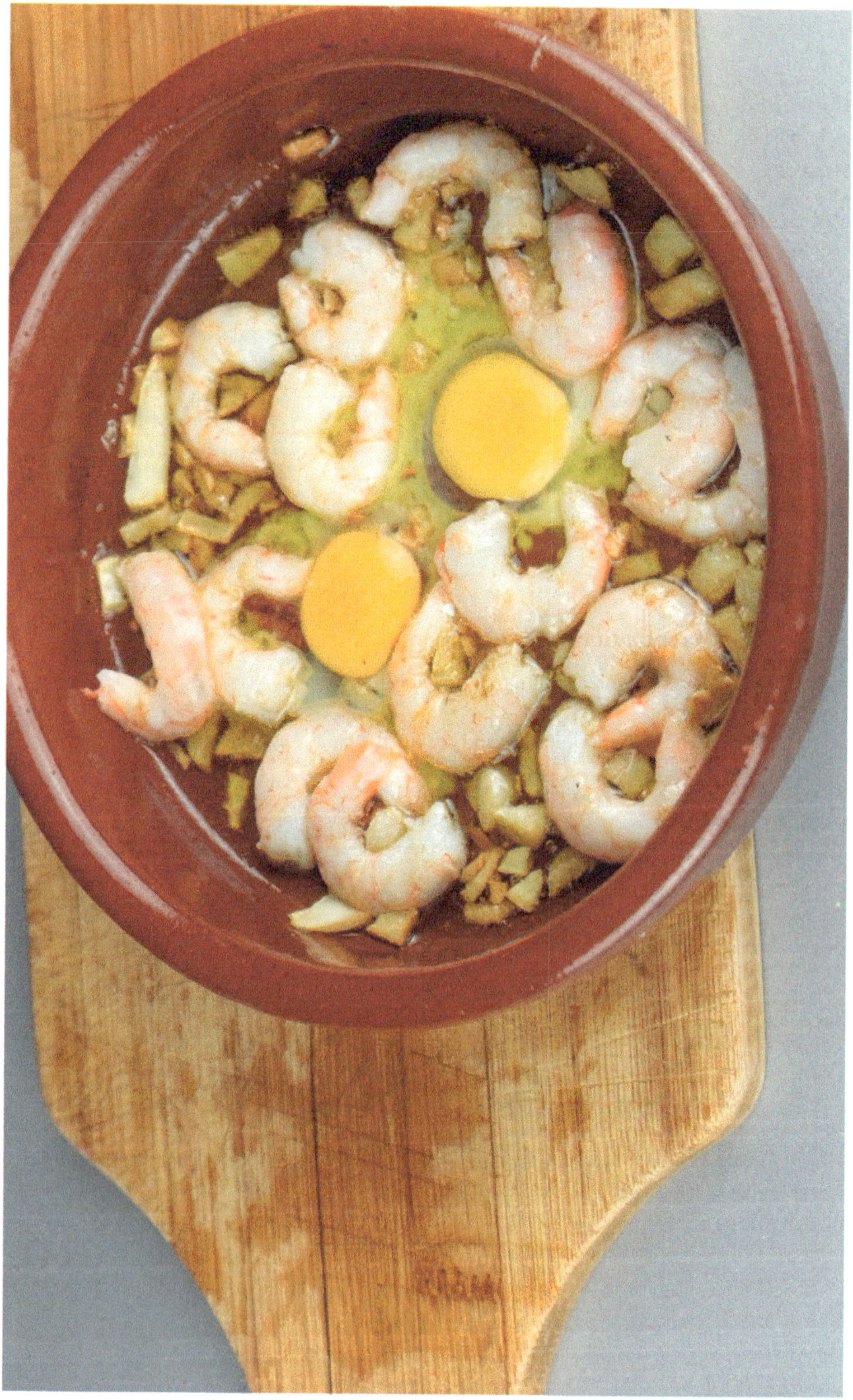

Recipe 34: Shrimps or Prawns in Garlic Olive Oil

Dive into the simple yet exquisite flavors of Shrimps or Prawns in Garlic Olive Oil, a Crock Pot dish that combines the succulence of seafood with the aromatic richness of garlic and olive oil. This recipe is an effortless way to create a luxurious and flavorful meal, perfect for seafood enthusiasts and gourmet cooks alike.

Servings: 4

Prepping Time: 10 minutes

Cook Time: 2 hours

Difficulty: Easy

Ingredients:

- 2 lbs shrimps or prawns, peeled and deveined
- 1/2 cup olive oil
- 6 cloves garlic, minced
- Salt and pepper to taste
- 1 lemon, for juice and zest
- Fresh parsley, chopped for garnish

Step-by-Step Preparation:

1. Combine shrimp or prawns with garlic, olive oil, salt, and pepper in the Crock Pot.
2. Cook on low for 2 hours until shrimp are pink and tender.
3. Just before serving, add lemon juice and zest.
4. Garnish with fresh parsley.

Nutritional Facts: (Per serving)

- Calories: 320
- Protein: 35g
- Carbohydrates: 2g
- Fat: 18g
- Sodium: 400mg

Enjoy Shrimp or Prawns in Garlic Olive Oil. This dish perfectly captures the essence of gourmet simplicity, making it an ideal choice for a special dinner or a delightful addition to your culinary repertoire.

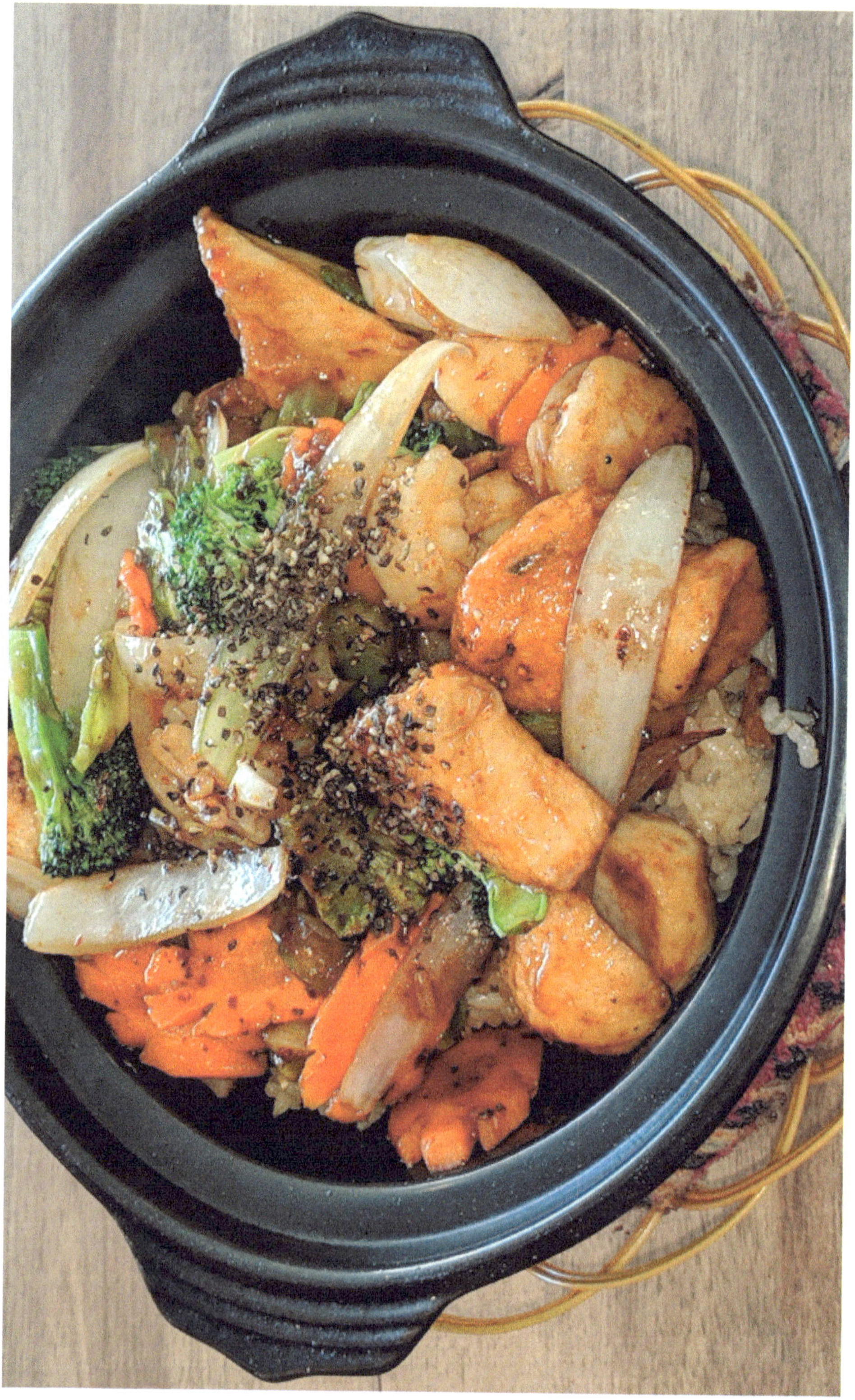

Recipe 35: Seafood Crock Pot

Embark on a culinary journey with Seafood Crock Pot, a delightful dish that quickly brings the sea's bounty to your table. This recipe combines a variety of seafood in a rich and flavorful broth, perfect for those who love the fresh tastes of the ocean in a convenient, slow-cooked meal.

Servings: 6

Prepping Time: 20 minutes

Cook Time: 4 hours

Difficulty: Medium

Ingredients:

- 1 lb shrimp, peeled and deveined
- 1 lb scallops
- 2 cups fish broth
- 1 can diced tomatoes
- 1 onion, chopped
- 2 garlic cloves, minced
- 1 tsp dried thyme
- 1 tsp dried basil
- Salt and pepper to taste

Step-by-Step Preparation:

1. Place shrimp, scallops, onion, and garlic in the Crock Pot.
2. Add diced tomatoes and fish broth.
3. Season with thyme, basil, salt, and pepper.
4. Cook on low for 4 hours, until seafood is cooked and flavors are melded.
5. Adjust seasoning as needed before serving.

Nutritional Facts: (Per serving)

- Calories: 220
- Protein: 35g
- Carbohydrates: 8g
- Fat: 4g
- Sodium: 500mg

Seafood Crock Pot is more than just a meal; it's an experience of comforting and luxurious flavors, making it perfect for a special occasion or a hearty family dinner.

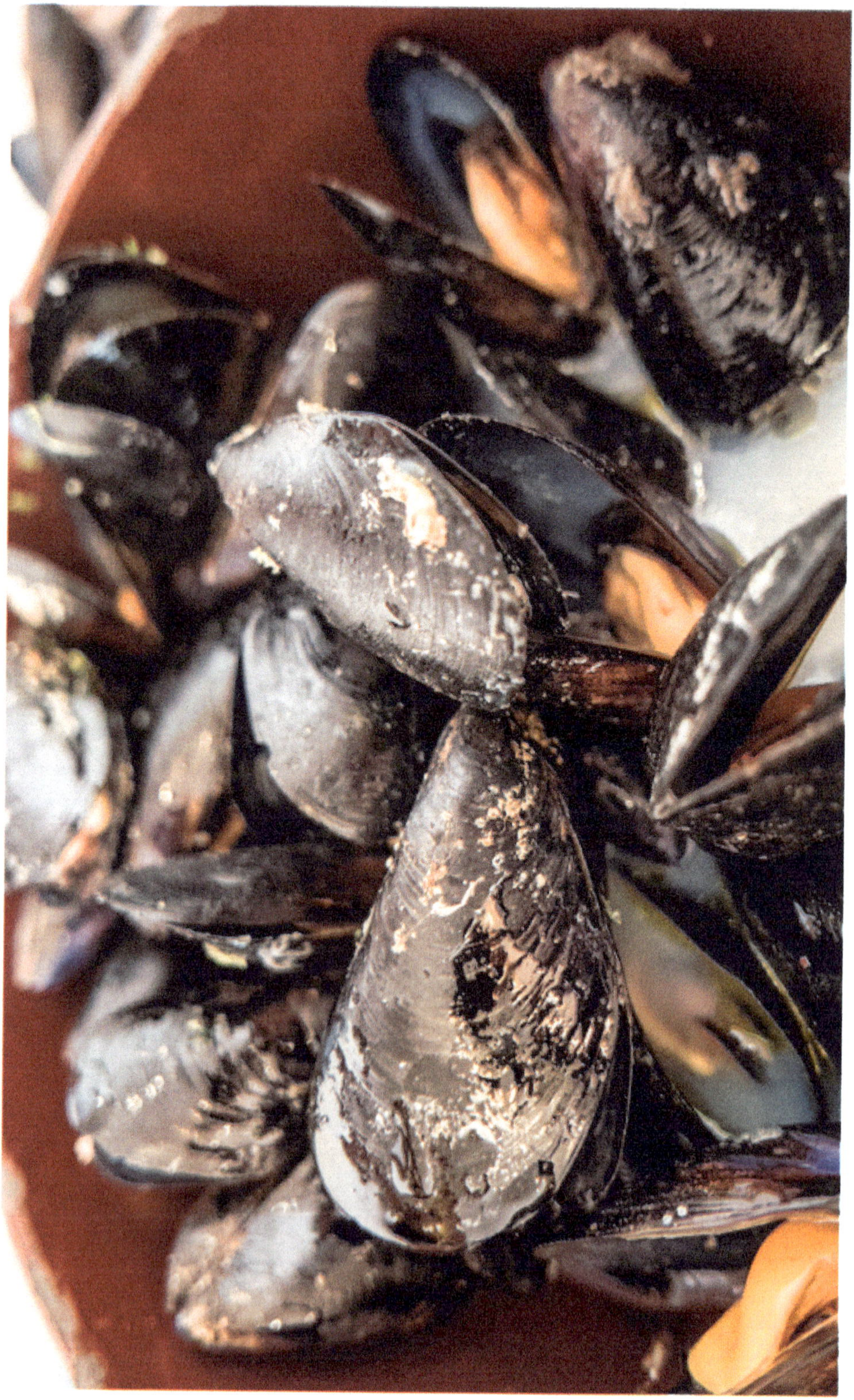

Recipe 36: Mussels in Crock Pot

"Mussels in Crock Pot" is a sumptuous seafood dish that turns the humble mussel into a star. This easy-to-prepare recipe brings the flavors of the sea right to your kitchen, offering a deliciously aromatic and tender experience that's perfect for seafood lovers and those seeking a simple yet elegant meal.

Servings: 4

Prepping Time: 10 minutes

Cook Time: 2-3 hours

Difficulty: Easy

Ingredients:

- 2 lbs fresh mussels, cleaned and debearded
- 1 cup white wine
- 1 onion, finely chopped
- 4 cloves garlic, minced
- 2 tomatoes, diced
- 1 lemon, juiced
- Fresh parsley, chopped for garnish
- Salt and pepper to taste

Step-by-Step Preparation:

1. Place mussels, onion, and garlic in the Crock Pot.
2. Add diced tomatoes and pour in white wine.
3. Season with salt, pepper, and lemon juice.
4. Cook on low for 2-3 hours until mussels open.
5. Discard any mussels that don't open. Garnish with fresh parsley before serving.

Nutritional Facts: (Per serving)

- Calories: 180
- Protein: 20g
- Carbohydrates: 9g
- Fat: 4g
- Sodium: 300mg

Enjoy the exquisite simplicity of "Mussels in Crock Pot," a dish that offers a delightful ocean taste, perfect for a cozy dinner or a special occasion, bringing a touch of elegance to your dining table.

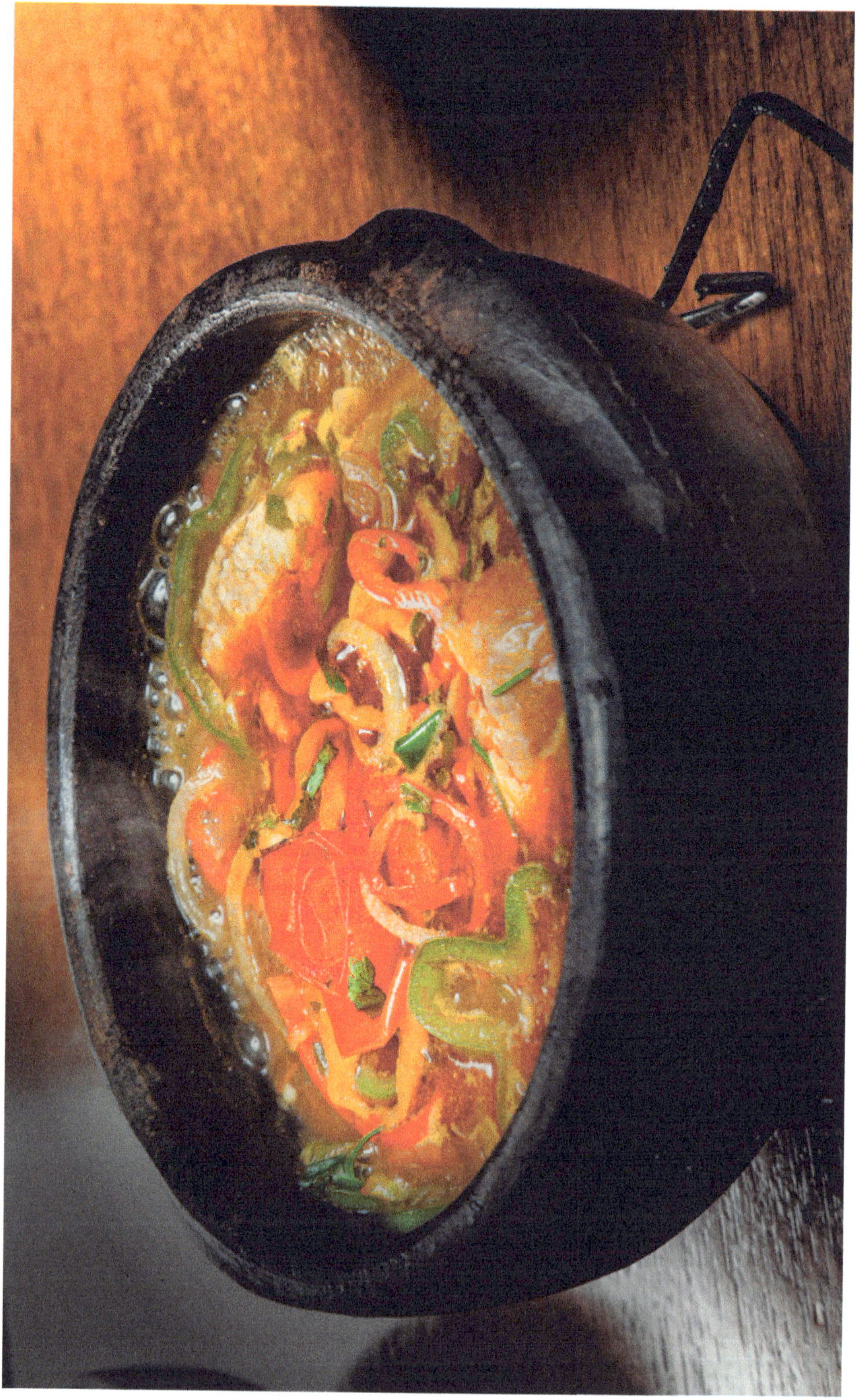

Recipe 37: Fish Stew in Crock Pot

Embark on a culinary adventure with this Fish Stew in a Crock Pot, where tender fish mingles with the comforting warmth of rice, flour, and pepper in olive oil. This recipe offers a harmonious blend of flavors, creating a hearty and nourishing meal perfect for seafood enthusiasts and home chefs.

Servings: 6

Prepping Time: 20 minutes

Cook Time: 4 hours

Difficulty: Medium

Ingredients:

- 2 lbs white fish fillets, cubed
- 1 cup rice
- 2 tbsp flour
- 1 bell pepper, chopped
- 4 cups fish broth
- 1 onion, diced
- 3 cloves garlic, minced
- 1/4 cup olive oil
- Salt and pepper to taste

Step-by-Step Preparation:

1. Coat fish cubes with flour, salt, and pepper.
2. Place the fish, rice, bell pepper, onion, and garlic in the Crock Pot.
3. Pour in fish broth and olive oil.
4. Cook on low for 4 hours until the fish is tender, and the stew is thickened.
5. Adjust seasoning as needed before serving.

Nutritional Facts: (Per serving)

- Calories: 300
- Protein: 30g
- Carbohydrates: 20g
- Fat: 10g
- Sodium: 300mg

Savor the rich and comforting flavors of this Fish Stew in Crock Pot, a dish that not only fills your home with a delightful aroma but also provides a satisfying and wholesome meal for any occasion.

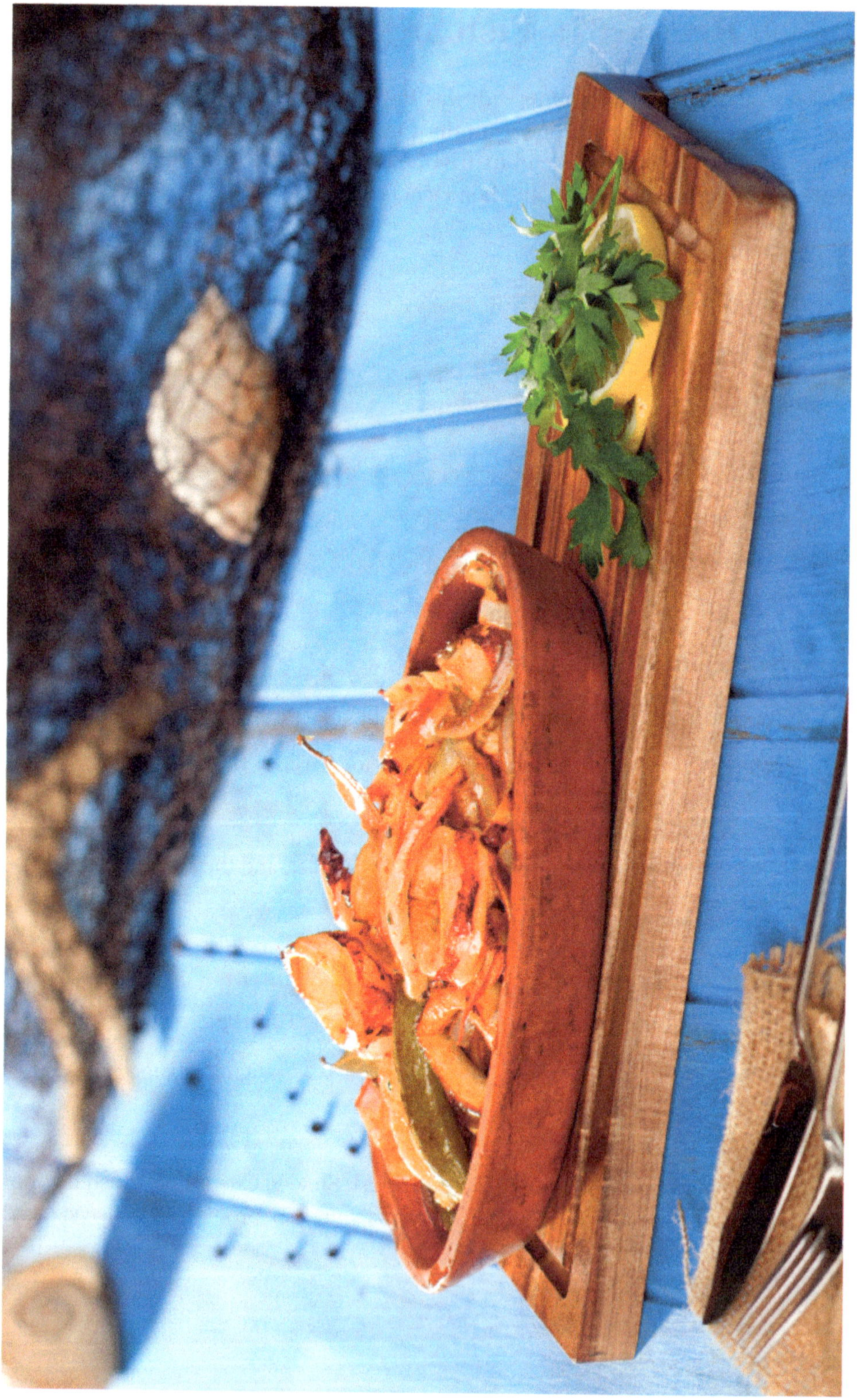

Recipe 38: Prawn, Squids, Fish and Mussels

Indulge in the luxurious flavors of the ocean with this Seafood Stew, a delectable Crock Pot dish featuring prawns, squids, fish, and mussels, all simmered in a rich olive oil base. This recipe is a seafood lover's dream, offering a sophisticated yet easy-to-prepare feast perfect for any special occasion or a lavish dinner.

Servings: 6

Prepping Time: 20 minutes

Cook Time: 4 hours

Difficulty: Medium

Ingredients:

- 1 lb prawns, peeled and deveined
- 1 lb squids, cleaned and sliced
- 2 lbs fish fillets, cubed
- 1 lb mussels, cleaned and debearded
- 1/4 cup olive oil
- 1 onion, chopped
- 3 cloves garlic, minced
- 1 cup white wine
- Salt and pepper to taste

Step-by-Step Preparation:

1. Place prawns, squids, fish, and mussels in the Crock Pot.
2. Add onion and garlic.
3. Pour in olive oil and white wine.
4. Season with salt and pepper.
5. Cook on low for 4 hours until seafood is tender and flavors are well combined.
6. Discard any mussels that do not open.

Nutritional Facts: (Per serving)

- Calories: 350
- Protein: 45g
- Carbohydrates: 5g
- Fat: 15g
- Sodium: 400mg

Enjoy the luxury of Seafood Stew, a dish that promises a delightful journey through the tastes of the sea, making any meal an extravagant and memorable experience.

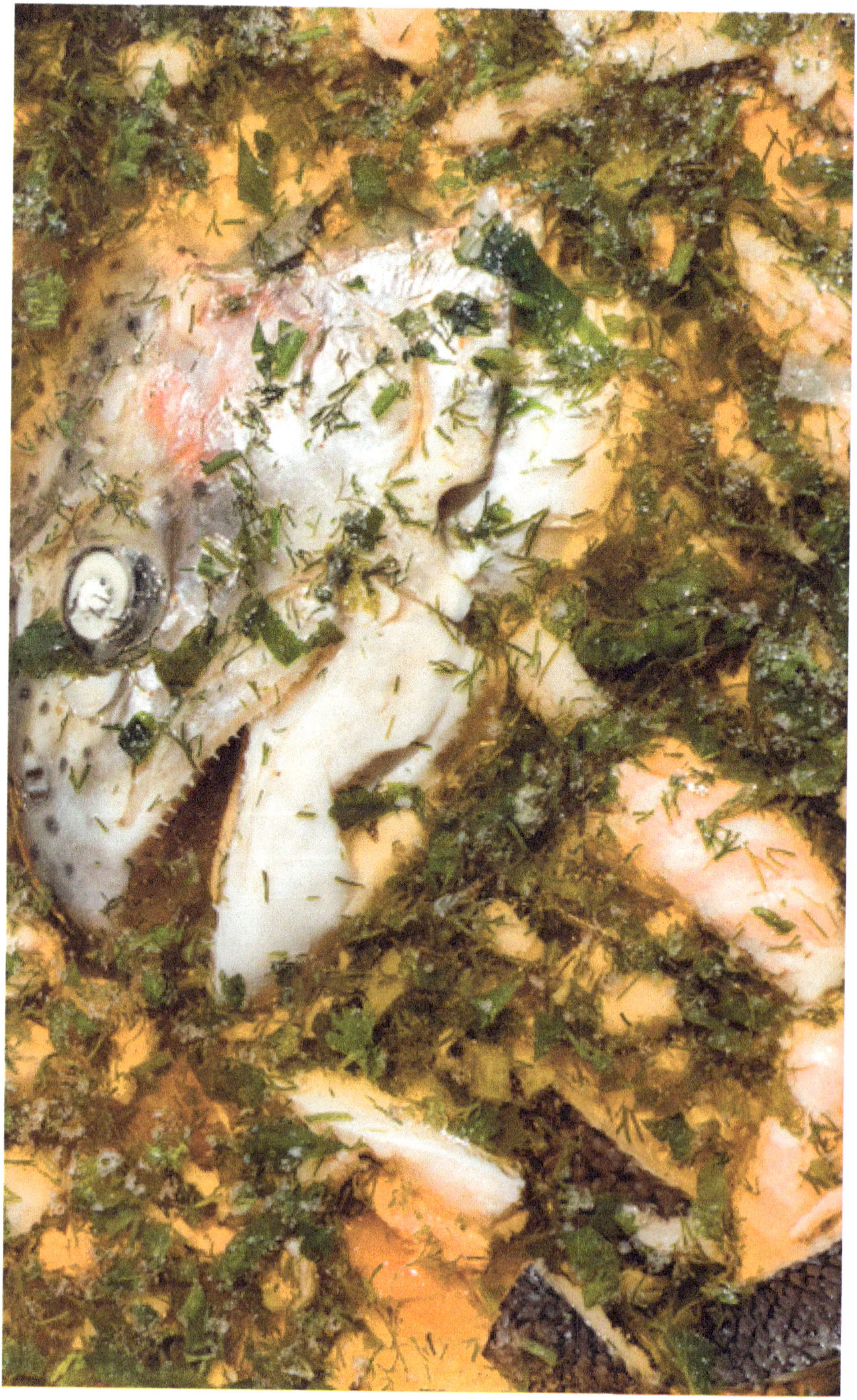

Recipe 39: Salmon Fish Broth

Delve into the comforting warmth of Salmon Fish Broth, a Crock Pot recipe that brings out the rich flavors of salmon in a delicate, savory broth. This dish is simple to prepare and a healthy choice for those seeking the nourishing benefits of a good fish broth, perfect for any day.

Servings: 4

Prepping Time: 15 minutes

Cook Time: 6 hours

Difficulty: Easy

Ingredients:

- 2 lbs salmon fillets
- 4 cups water
- 1 onion, chopped
- 2 carrots, chopped
- 2 celery stalks, chopped
- 1 bay leaf
- Salt and pepper to taste

Step-by-Step Preparation:

1. Place salmon fillets in the Crock Pot.
2. Add water, onion, carrots, celery, and bay leaf.
3. Season with salt and pepper.
4. Cook on low for 6 hours.
5. Strain the broth and serve hot.

Nutritional Facts: (Per serving)

- Calories: 200
- Protein: 22g
- Carbohydrates: 5g
- Fat: 10g
- Sodium: 75mg

Savor the simplicity and elegance of Salmon Fish Broth. This dish not only soothes the soul but also provides a light yet satisfying meal, ideal for those who appreciate seafood's subtle and healthful pleasures.

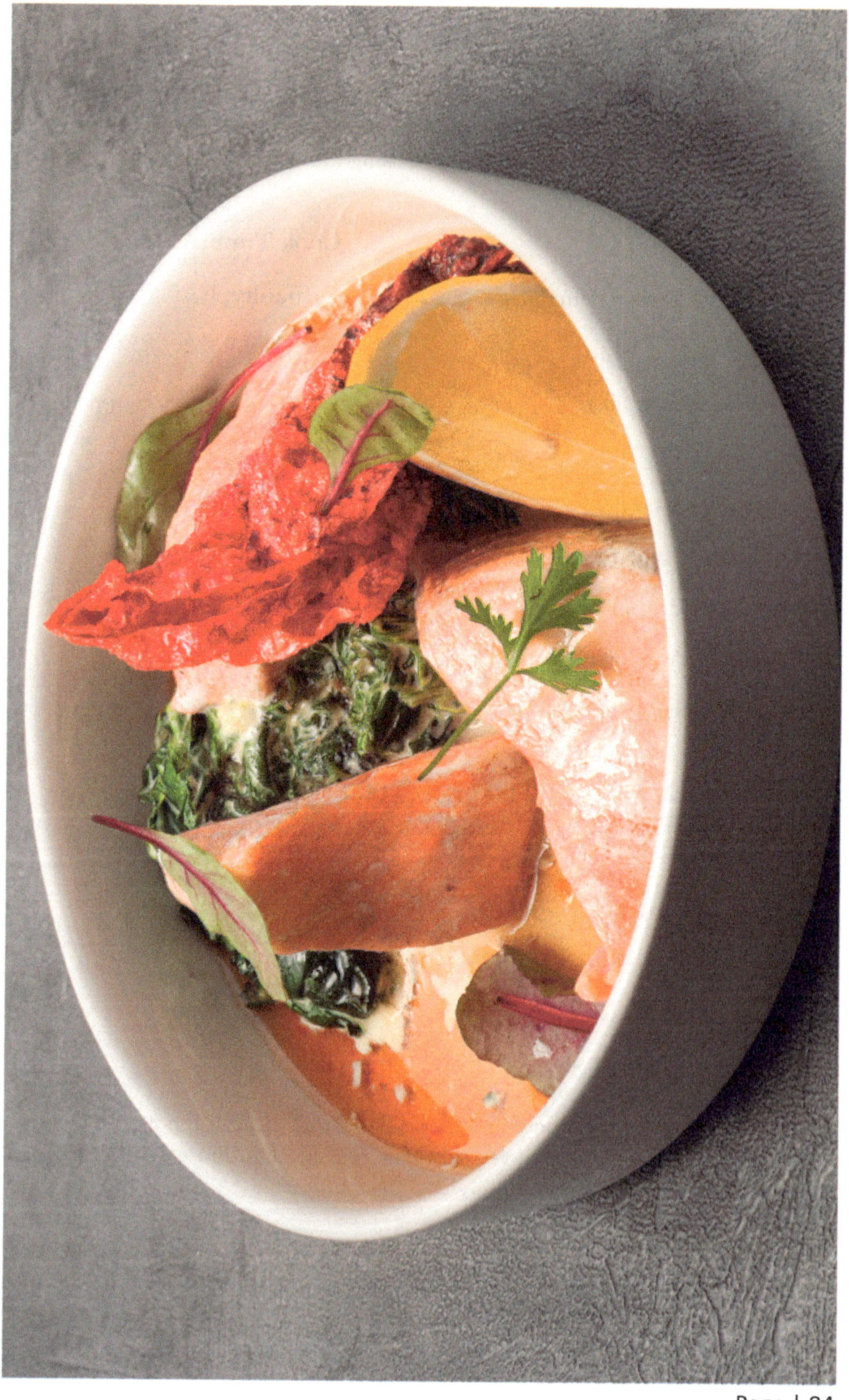

Recipe 40: Salmon With Spinach and Teriyaki Sauce

Embark on a culinary journey with "Salmon with Spinach and Teriyaki Sauce," a Crock Pot dish that beautifully marries the rich flavors of salmon with the earthiness of spinach, all enhanced by a sweet and savory teriyaki glaze. This recipe is perfect for those seeking a delicious, healthy, easy-to-prepare seafood meal.

Servings: 4

Prepping Time: 15 minutes

Cook Time: 2-3 hours

Difficulty: Easy

Ingredients:

- 4 salmon fillets
- 4 cups fresh spinach
- 1/2 cup teriyaki sauce
- 2 cloves garlic, minced
- 1 tbsp ginger, grated
- Salt and pepper to taste

Step-by-Step Preparation:

1. Place salmon fillets in the Crock Pot.
2. Season with salt, pepper, garlic, and ginger.
3. Pour teriyaki sauce over the salmon.
4. Add spinach around the salmon.
5. Cook on low for 2-3 hours until salmon is cooked through.
6. Serve the salmon and spinach with extra teriyaki sauce drizzled on top.

Nutritional Facts: (Per serving)

- Calories: 300
- Protein: 23g
- Carbohydrates: 10g
- Fat: 15g
- Sodium: 900mg

Enjoy "Salmon with Spinach and Teriyaki Sauce," a dish that offers a delightful fusion of flavors, perfect for a special dinner or a nutritious weekday meal, bringing a touch of gourmet to your regular dining experience.

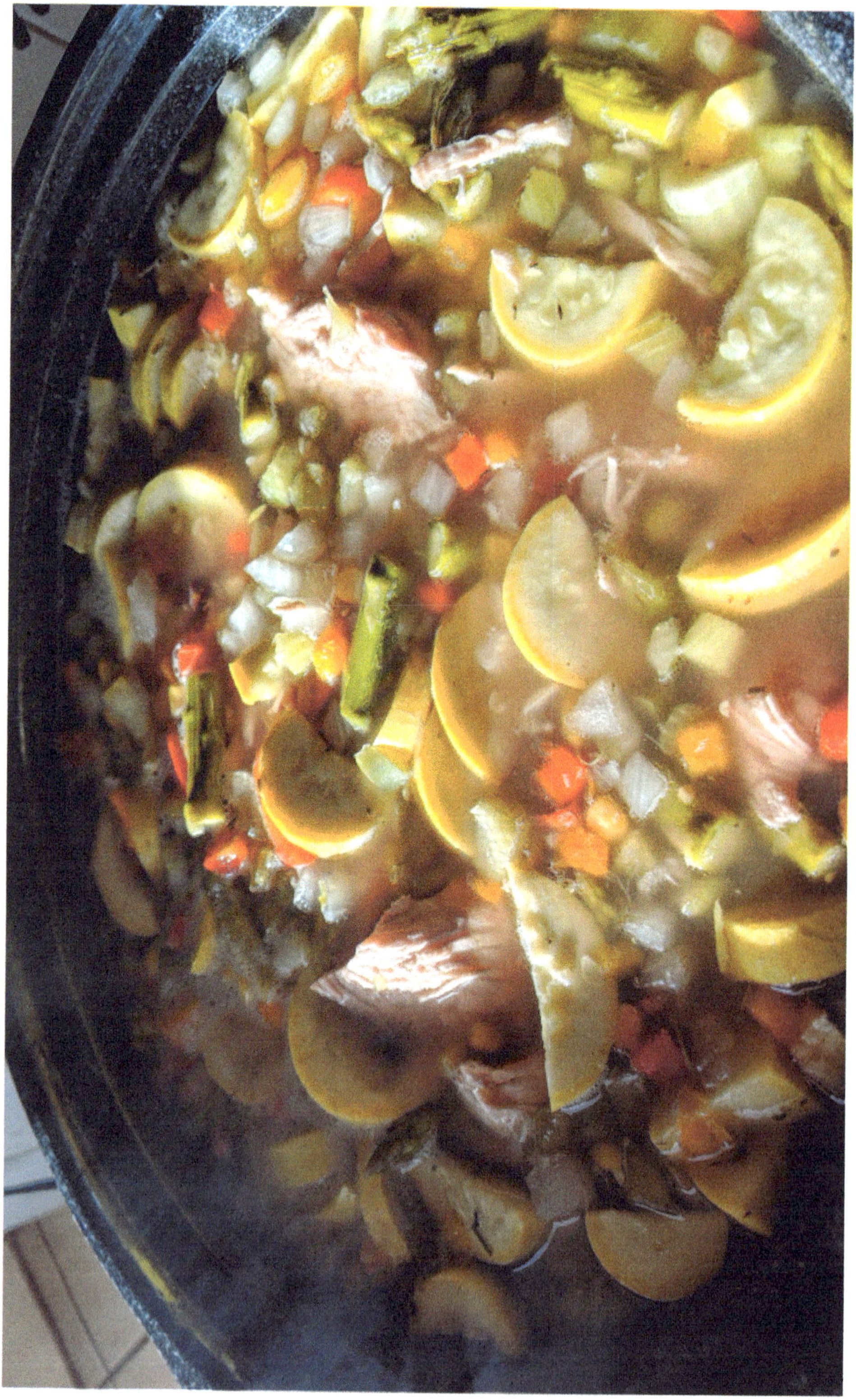

Chapter 05: Soothing Soup Sensations

Recipe 41: Chicken Vegetable Soup

"Chicken Vegetable Soup" in a Crock Pot is a classic, comforting dish perfect for any season. This recipe combines tender chicken with various vegetables, creating a healthy and hearty soup that's both easy to make and delightful to eat, ideal for those looking for a nourishing meal with minimal fuss.

Servings: 6

Prepping Time: 20 minutes

Cook Time: 6-8 hours

Difficulty: Easy

Ingredients:

- 2 boneless chicken breasts
- 2 carrots, sliced
- 2 celery stalks, chopped
- 1 onion, chopped
- 3 cloves garlic, minced
- 4 cups chicken broth
- 1 tsp dried thyme
- Salt and pepper to taste

Step-by-Step Preparation:

1. Place chicken breasts at the bottom of the Crock Pot.
2. Add carrots, celery, onion, and garlic.
3. Pour in chicken broth and season with thyme, salt, and pepper.
4. Cook on low for 6-8 hours.
5. Shred the chicken before serving.

Nutritional Facts: (Per serving)

- Calories: 120
- Protein: 15g
- Carbohydrates: 8g
- Fat: 3g
- Sodium: 500mg

Enjoy this Chicken Vegetable Soup, a warm and wholesome dish perfect for cozy nights in or as a comforting meal to share with family and friends, embodying the essence of home-cooked goodness.

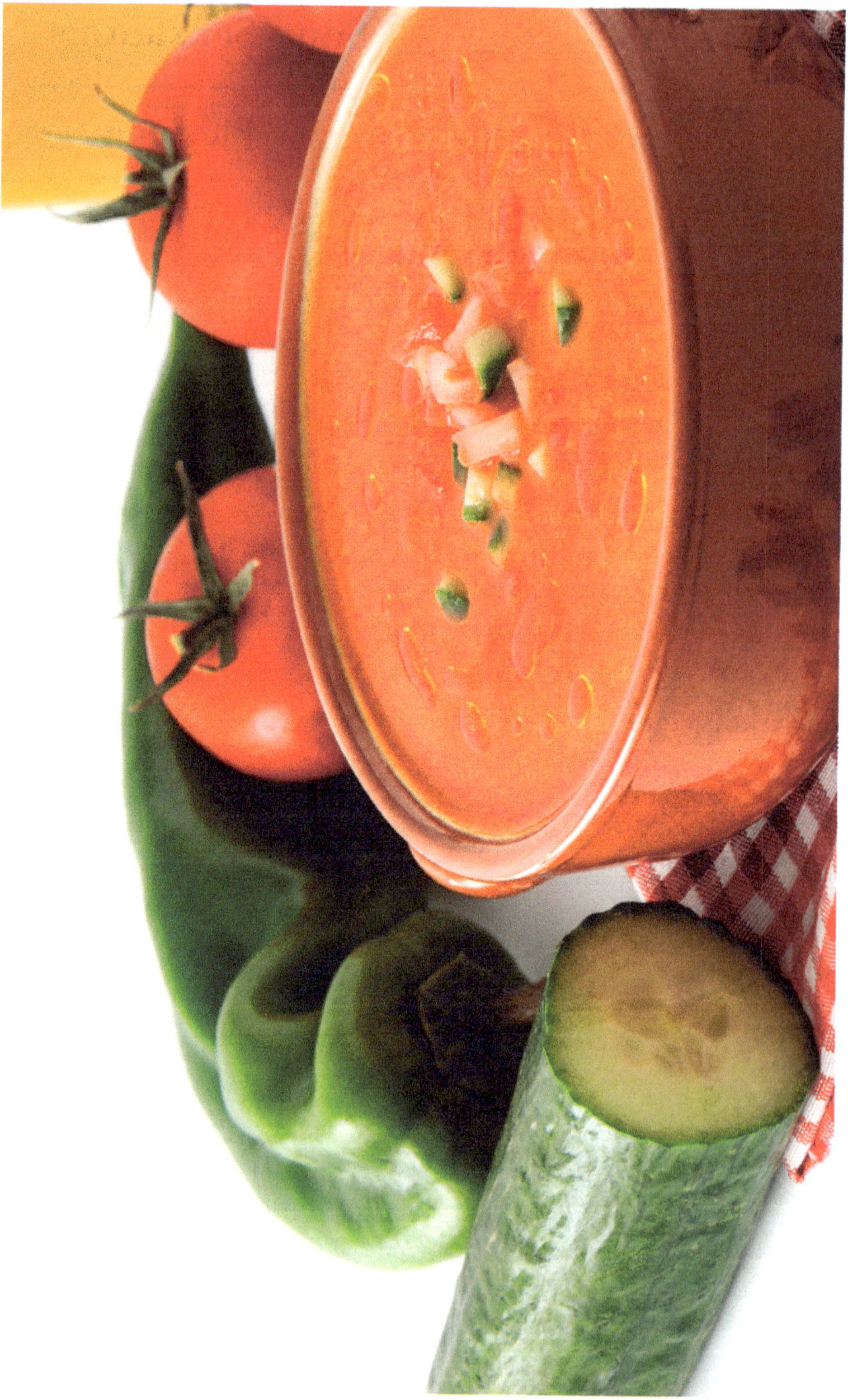

Recipe 42: Gazpacho Soup

Experience the flavors of Spain with this delightful Gazpacho Soup, perfect for any season. A refreshing blend of fresh vegetables, it's a healthy choice for a light meal or appetizer.

Servings: 6

Prepping Time: 15 minutes

Cook Time: 4 hours (Low heat in Crock Pot)

Difficulty: Easy

Ingredients:

- ✓ 1 kg ripe tomatoes, roughly chopped
- ✓ 1 cucumber, peeled and chopped
- ✓ 1 bell pepper, seeded and chopped
- ✓ 1 small red onion, chopped
- ✓ 2 cloves garlic, minced
- ✓ 3 tbsp olive oil
- ✓ 2 tbsp red wine vinegar
- ✓ Salt and pepper to taste
- ✓ Fresh basil leaves for garnish

Step-by-Step Preparation:

1. Combine tomatoes, cucumber, bell pepper, onion, and garlic in the Crock Pot.
2. Stir in olive oil and red wine vinegar. Season with salt and pepper.
3. Cover and cook on low for 4 hours, allowing flavors to meld.
4. Blend the mixture until smooth, and adjust the seasoning if necessary.
5. Chill in the refrigerator for at least 1 hour.
6. Serve cold, garnished with fresh basil.

Nutritional Facts: (Per serving)

- ❖ Calories: 120
- ❖ Fat: 7g
- ❖ Carbohydrates: 13g
- ❖ Protein: 2g
- ❖ Fiber: 3g
- ❖ Sugar: 8g

Conclude your day with a bowl of this refreshing Gazpacho Soup. It's a perfect dish to cool down on a warm day or add a summer splash to your winter meals. Enjoy the simplicity and freshness in every spoonful!

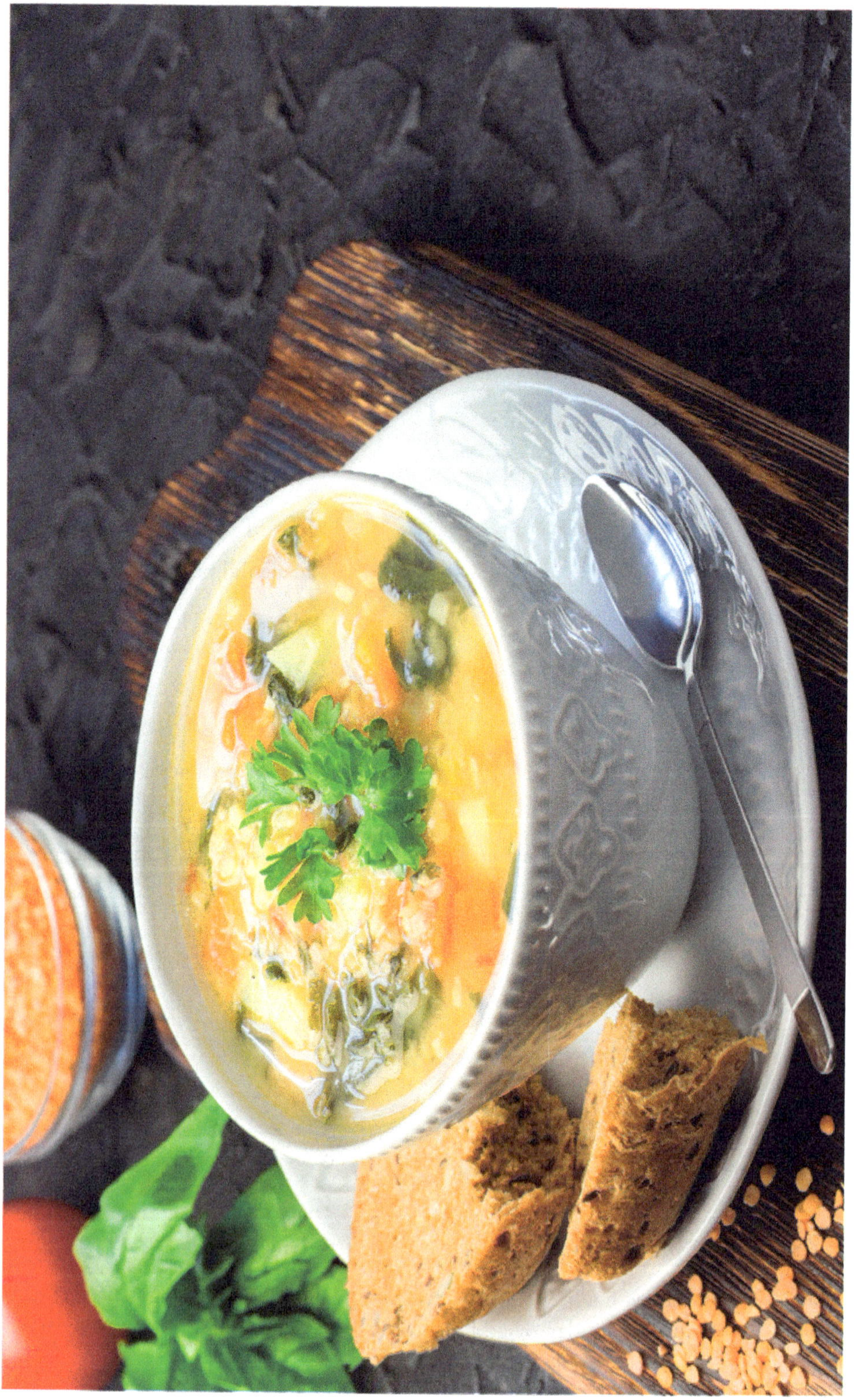

Recipe 43: Red Lentil Vegetable Soup

Savor the nourishing goodness of Detox Crock Pot Red Lentil Vegetable Soup. This hearty, wholesome recipe combines red lentils with a medley of vegetables, creating a comforting and detoxifying meal perfect for health-conscious food lovers.

Servings: 8

Prepping Time: 20 minutes

Cook Time: 6 hours (Low heat in Crock Pot)

Difficulty: Easy

Ingredients:

- 1 cup red lentils, rinsed
- 2 carrots, chopped
- 2 celery stalks, chopped
- 1 onion, diced
- 3 garlic cloves, minced
- 1 red bell pepper, chopped
- 1 zucchini, chopped
- 1 can (14 oz) diced tomatoes
- 4 cups vegetable broth
- 1 tsp turmeric
- 1 tsp cumin
- Salt and pepper to taste
- Fresh parsley for garnish

Step-by-Step Preparation:

1. Place red lentils, carrots, celery, onion, garlic, bell pepper, and zucchini in the Crock Pot.
2. Add diced tomatoes and vegetable broth.
3. Season with turmeric, cumin, salt, and pepper.
4. Stir well to combine all ingredients.
5. Cover and cook on low heat for 6 hours.
6. Check consistency and seasoning and adjust if necessary.
7. Serve hot, garnished with fresh parsley.

Nutritional Facts: (Per serving)

- Calories: 160
- Fat: 1g
- Carbohydrates: 29g
- Protein: 9g
- Fiber: 6g
- Sugar: 5g

Indulge in the warmth and comfort of this Detox Crock Pot Red Lentil Vegetable Soup. Whether you want to cleanse your body or enjoy a delicious, healthy meal, this soup is the perfect choice for a satisfying and rejuvenating experience.

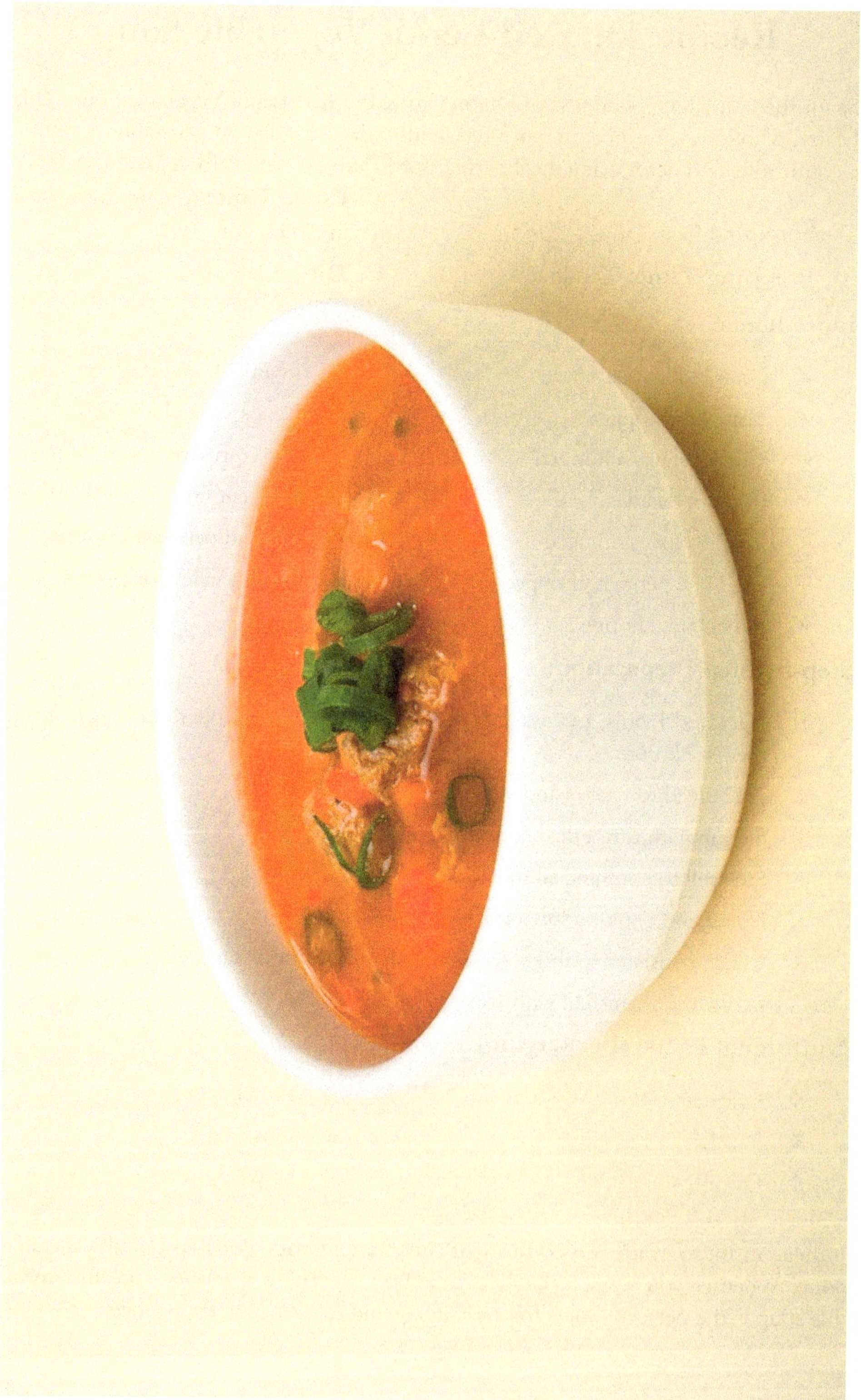

Recipe 44: Beef, Vegetable, and Tomato Soup

Indulge in the hearty and comforting flavors of Beef, Vegetable, and Tomato Soup. This Crock Pot recipe perfectly combines tender beef, fresh vegetables, and rich tomatoes, creating a delicious and nourishing meal that's ideal for cozy evenings.

Servings: 6

Prepping Time: 20 minutes

Cook Time: 8 hours (Low heat in Crock Pot)

Difficulty: Medium

Ingredients:

- 500g beef stew meat, cubed
- 4 carrots, sliced
- 400g canned diced tomatoes
- 2 celery stalks, chopped
- 4 spring onions, chopped
- 3 garlic cloves, minced
- 4 cups beef broth
- 1 tsp dried basil
- 1 tsp dried thyme
- Salt and pepper to taste

Step-by-Step Preparation:

1. Brown the beef cubes in a skillet over medium heat, then transfer to the Crock Pot.
2. Add sliced carrots, diced tomatoes, chopped celery, and spring onions.
3. Stir in minced garlic, beef broth, basil, and thyme.
4. Season with salt and pepper.
5. Cover and cook on low heat for 8 hours.
6. Check the tenderness of the beef and vegetables, and adjust seasoning if necessary.
7. Serve hot and enjoy.

Nutritional Facts: (Per serving)

- Calories: 250
- Fat: 8g
- Carbohydrates: 15g
- Protein: 28g
- Fiber: 3g
- Sugar: 5g

This Beef, Vegetable, and Tomato Soup is not just a meal, it's a comforting embrace in a bowl. Perfect for winding down after a long day, each spoonful offers flavor and warmth, making it a great addition to your recipe collection.

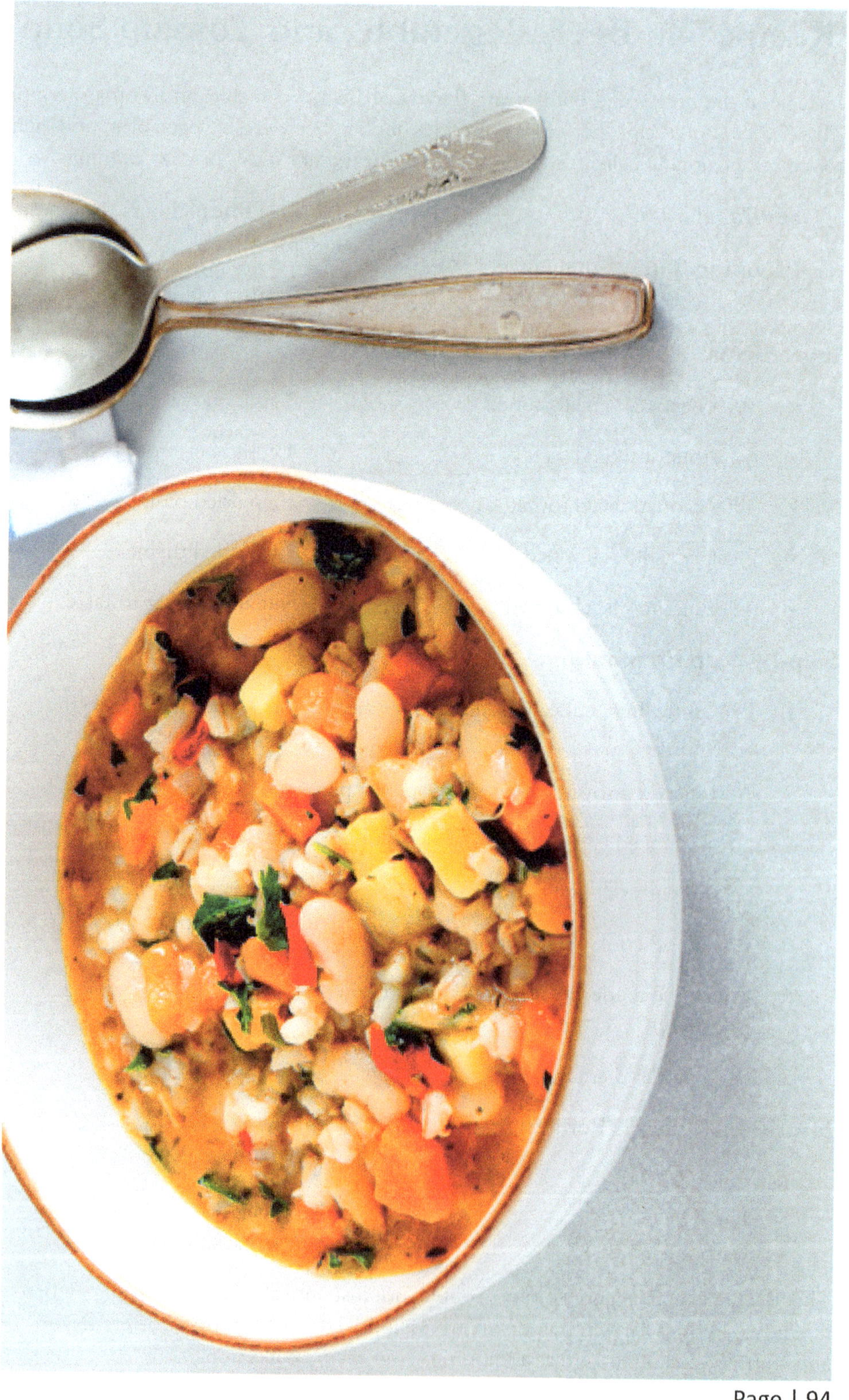

Recipe 45: Pearl Barley Beans Soup

Delight in the earthy and wholesome flavors of Pearl Barley and Bean Soup, enriched with squash, pumpkin, potato, and carrot. This Crock Pot recipe is a symphony of textures and tastes, offering a comforting and nutritious meal perfect for any day.

Servings: 6

Prepping Time: 15 minutes

Cook Time: 6 hours (Low heat in Crock Pot)

Difficulty: Easy

Ingredients:

- 1 cup pearl barley, rinsed
- 1 cup beans (cannellini or navy), soaked overnight
- 2 cups squash, cubed
- 1 cup pumpkin, cubed
- 2 potatoes, cubed
- 2 carrots, sliced
- 6 cups vegetable broth
- 1 onion, chopped
- 2 garlic cloves, minced
- 1 tsp thyme
- Salt and pepper to taste

Step-by-Step Preparation:

1. Place soaked beans and rinsed pearl barley in the Crock Pot.
2. Add cubed squash, pumpkin, potatoes, and sliced carrots.
3. Pour in the vegetable broth.
4. Add chopped onion, minced garlic, and thyme.
5. Season with salt and pepper.
6. Stir well to combine all ingredients.
7. Cover and cook on low heat for 6 hours.
8. Check the tenderness of vegetables and barley, and adjust seasoning if needed.
9. Serve warm and enjoy.

Nutritional Facts: (Per serving)

- Calories: 220
- Fat: 1g
- Carbohydrates: 45g
- Protein: 8g
- Fiber: 10g
- Sugar: 5g

This Pearl Barley and Bean Soup with squash, pumpkin, potato, and carrot perfectly blends heartiness and health. Whether you're seeking comfort on a chilly day or a nutritious meal for your family, this soup is a delightful choice that's sure to please.

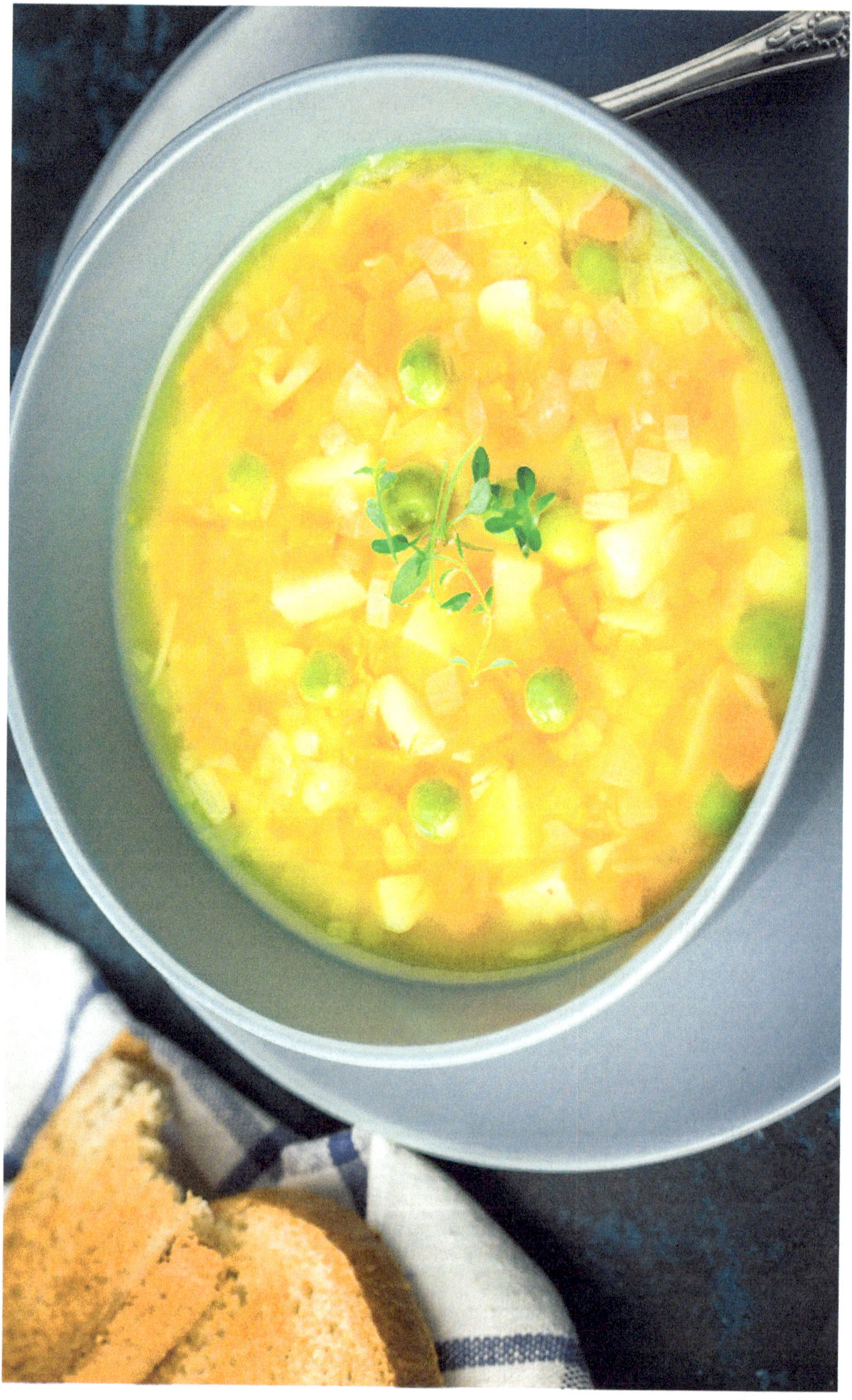

Recipe 46: Turmeric Split Pea Soup

Embark on a culinary journey with the vibrant and aromatic Turmeric Split Pea Soup. This Crock Pot creation combines the earthy flavors of split peas with the warm, golden hues of turmeric, creating a soup that's not only delicious but also brimming with health benefits.

Servings: 6

Prepping Time: 10 minutes

Cook Time: 8 hours (Low heat in Crock Pot)

Difficulty: Easy

Ingredients:

- 2 cups dried split peas, rinsed
- 1 large onion, chopped
- 2 carrots, diced
- 2 celery stalks, diced
- 3 garlic cloves, minced
- 1 tsp ground turmeric
- 6 cups vegetable broth
- Salt and pepper to taste
- Fresh parsley, chopped (for garnish)

Step-by-Step Preparation:

1. Place rinsed split peas in the Crock Pot.
2. Add chopped onion, diced carrots, and celery.
3. Stir in minced garlic and ground turmeric.
4. Pour in vegetable broth and season with salt and pepper.
5. Stir well to combine all ingredients.
6. Cover and cook on low heat for 8 hours.
7. Check the consistency and adjust the seasoning if needed.
8. Serve hot, garnished with fresh parsley.

Nutritional Facts: (Per serving)

- Calories: 230
- Fat: 1g
- Carbohydrates: 42g
- Protein: 16g
- Fiber: 16g
- Sugar: 6g

This Turmeric Split Pea Soup is a testament to simplicity and flavor, making it a must-try for soup enthusiasts. Its soothing warmth and nutritional richness make it an excellent choice for a comforting dinner or a healthy lunch. Enjoy each spoonful of this golden, hearty delight!

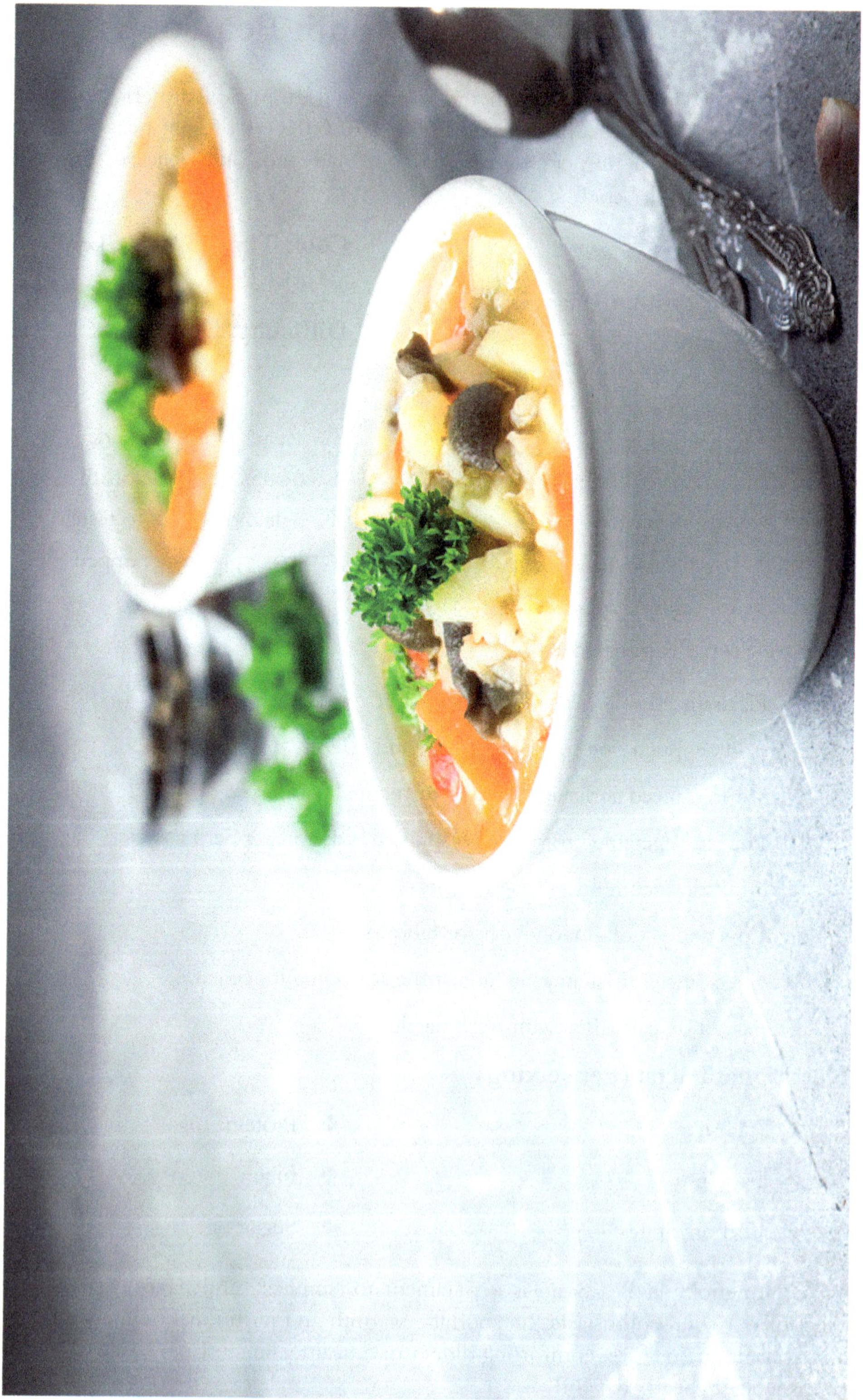

Recipe 47: Mushroom Barley Soup

Savor the earthy goodness of Vegan Mushroom Barley Soup, a delightful blend of hearty barley and flavorful mushrooms. This Crock Pot recipe is a vegan delight, offering a comforting and nutritious meal perfect for any day, especially during the cooler months.

Servings: 6

Prepping Time: 15 minutes

Cook Time: 4 hours (High heat in Crock Pot)

Difficulty: Easy

Ingredients:

- 1 cup pearl barley, rinsed
- 2 cups mushrooms, sliced
- 1 onion, diced
- 2 garlic cloves, minced
- 2 carrots, diced
- 2 celery stalks, diced
- 6 cups vegetable broth
- 1 tsp dried thyme
- 1 bay leaf
- Salt and pepper to taste

Step-by-Step Preparation:

1. Place rinsed pearl barley and sliced mushrooms in the Crock Pot.
2. Add diced onion, minced garlic, carrots, and celery.
3. Pour in vegetable broth.
4. Season with dried thyme, bay leaf, salt, and pepper.
5. Stir to combine all ingredients.
6. Cover and cook on high heat for 4 hours.
7. Remove bay leaf and adjust seasoning if needed.
8. Serve hot and enjoy.

Nutritional Facts: (Per serving)

- Calories: 180
- Fat: 1g
- Carbohydrates: 39g
- Protein: 6g
- Fiber: 9g
- Sugar: 5g

This Vegan Mushroom Barley Soup is a warming and satisfying dish for those seeking a healthy yet hearty meal. Its robust flavors and simple preparation make it an ideal choice for novice and experienced cooks. Relish the blend of textures and tastes in every spoonful!

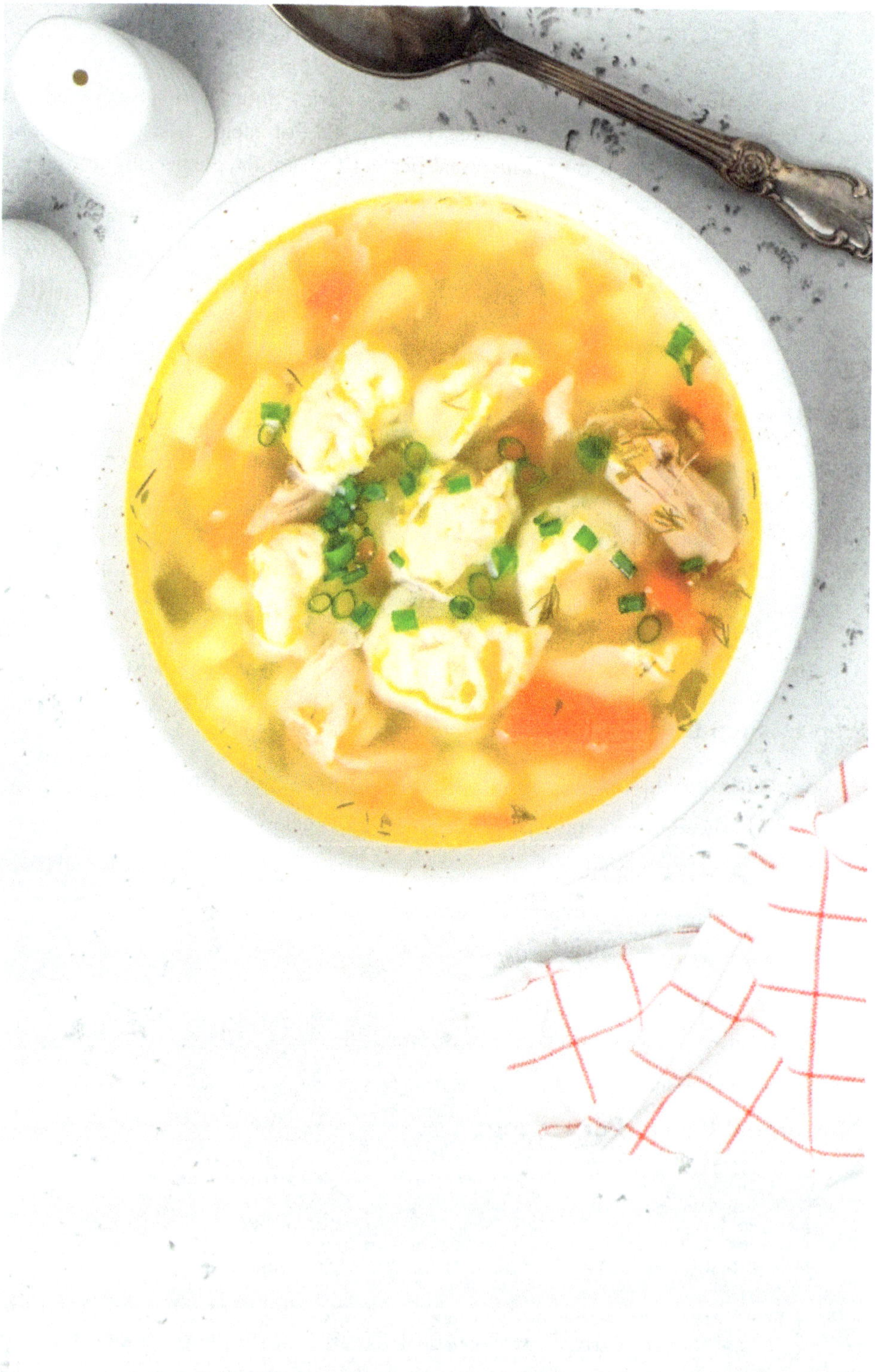

Recipe 48: Chicken Soup With Dumplings

Warm your soul with a classic comfort dish, Chicken Soup with Dumplings. This Crock Pot recipe brings together tender chicken, vegetables, and soft, pillowy dumplings in a savory broth, creating a meal as nourishing as it is delicious, perfect for any day with a touch of coziness.

Servings: 6
Prepping Time: 20 minutes
Cook Time: 6 hours (Low heat in Crock Pot)
Difficulty: Medium

Ingredients:

- 500g boneless, skinless chicken breasts
- 1 onion, chopped
- 2 carrots, sliced
- 2 celery stalks, sliced
- 4 cups chicken broth
- 1 tsp thyme
- 1 tsp parsley
- Salt and pepper to taste
- **For Dumplings:**
- 1 cup all-purpose flour
- 2 tsp baking powder
- ½ tsp salt
- ½ cup milk
- 2 tbsp unsalted butter, melted

Step-by-Step Preparation:

1. Place chicken, onion, carrots, and celery in the Crock Pot.
2. Add thyme, parsley, salt, and pepper to chicken broth.
3. Cover and cook on low for 5 hours.
4. Mix flour, baking powder, and salt in a bowl for dumplings. Stir in milk and melted butter to form a soft dough.
5. Drop spoonfuls of dumpling dough on top of the soup.
6. Cover and cook for an additional 1 hour until the dumplings are cooked.
7. Shred the chicken in the pot and stir gently.
8. Serve the soup hot, with dumplings.

Nutritional Facts: (Per serving)

- Calories: 300
- Fat: 6g
- Carbohydrates: 30g
- Protein: 28g
- Fiber: 2g
- Sugar: 3g

Chicken Soup with Dumplings is the perfect recipe to bring comfort and warmth to your dining table. It's a hearty meal that combines the homely goodness of chicken soup with the delightful surprise of dumplings, making it a favorite for kids and adults. Enjoy this cozy, fulfilling meal with your loved ones!

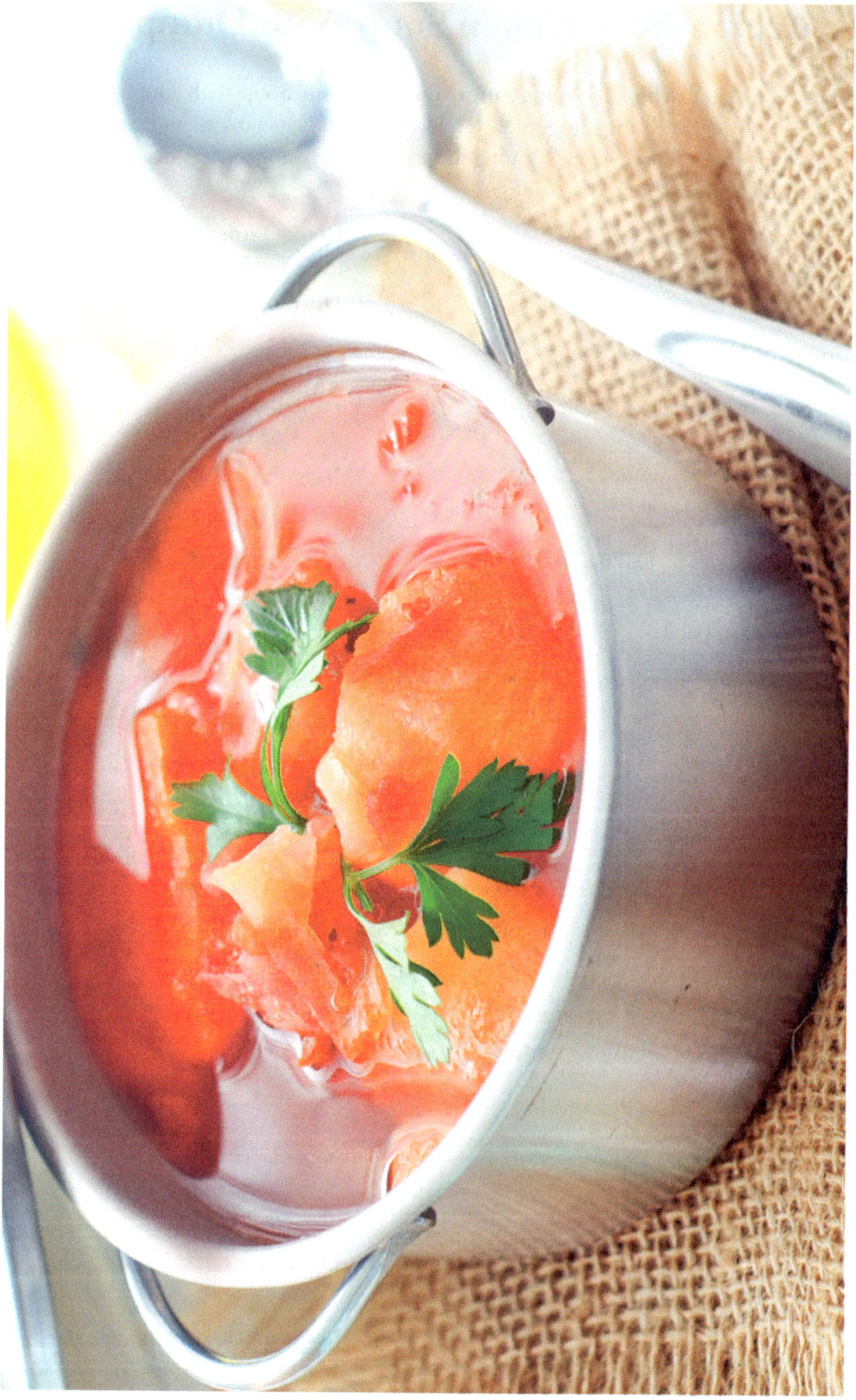

Recipe 49: Veal Stew Soup

Dive into the rich and hearty world of Veal Stew Soup, a Crock Pot masterpiece that perfectly marries tender veal with a medley of fresh vegetables. This soul-warming soup is not just a meal but an experience, offering a symphony of flavors that comfort and satisfy with every spoonful.

Servings: 6

Prepping Time: 20 minutes

Cook Time: 8 hours (Low heat in Crock Pot)

Difficulty: Medium

Ingredients:

- 1 kg veal, cubed
- 2 carrots, chopped
- 2 potatoes, cubed
- 1 onion, diced
- 2 celery stalks, chopped
- 3 garlic cloves, minced
- 4 cups beef broth
- 1 can (14 oz) diced tomatoes
- 1 tsp rosemary
- 1 tsp thyme
- Salt and pepper to taste

Step-by-Step Preparation:

1. Brown the veal cubes in a skillet, then transfer to the Crock Pot.
2. Add chopped carrots, potatoes, onion, and celery.
3. Mix in minced garlic, beef broth, and diced tomatoes.
4. Season with rosemary, thyme, salt, and pepper.
5. Stir to combine all the ingredients.
6. Cover and cook on low heat for 8 hours.
7. Check the tenderness of the meat and vegetables, and adjust seasoning if necessary.
8. Serve the stew hot and savor every bite.

Nutritional Facts: (Per serving)

- Calories: 360
- Fat: 10g
- Carbohydrates: 30g
- Protein: 35g
- Fiber: 4g
- Sugar: 5g

This Veal Stew Soup is the epitome of comfort food, ideal for those chilly days or whenever you crave a wholesome, fulfilling meal. Its blend of tender meat and vegetables, simmered to perfection, makes it a must-try for anyone looking to satisfy their soul with good food.

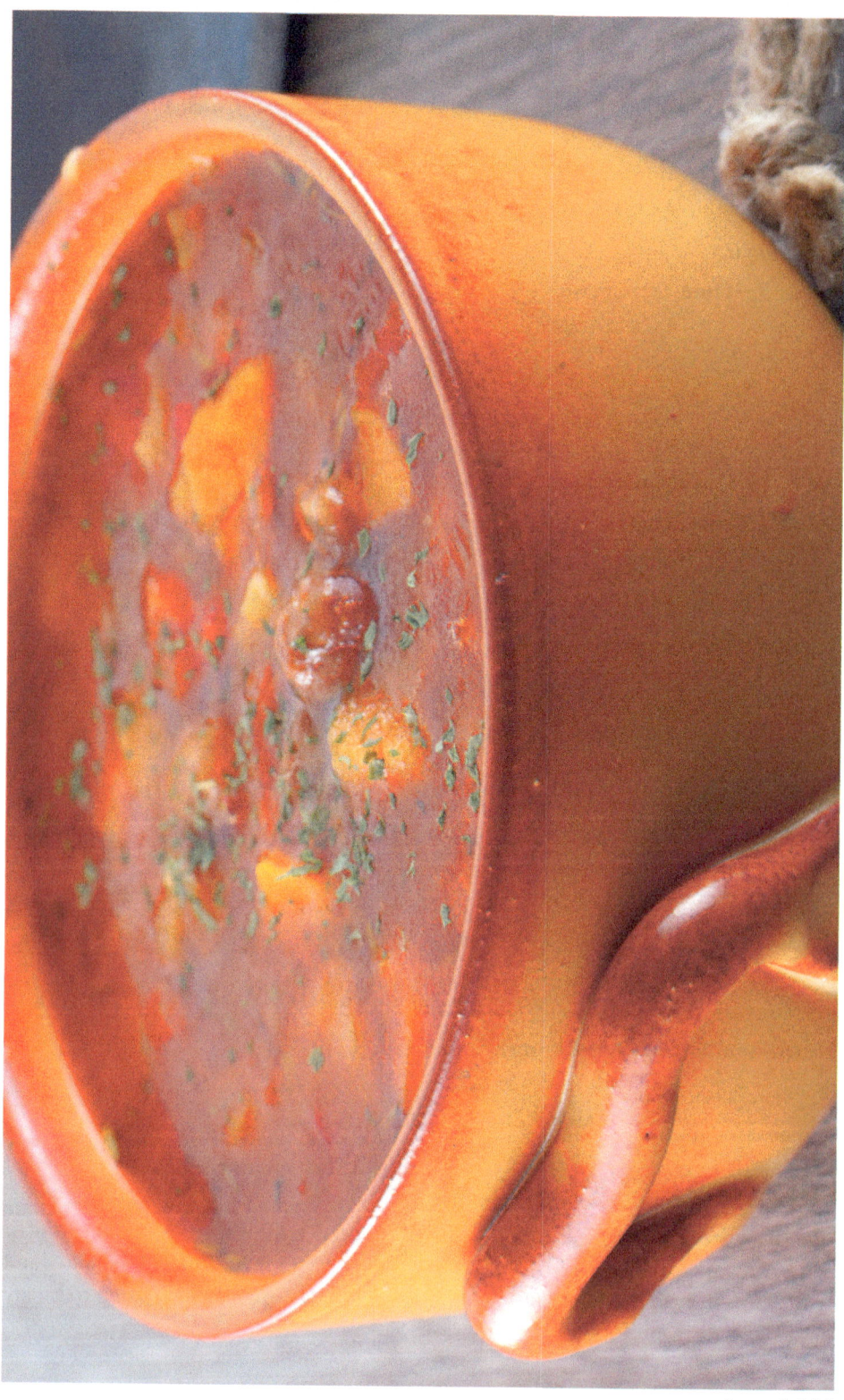

Recipe 50: Soup With Beans, Tomato and Bread

Delve into the rustic charm of soup with beans, tomatoes, and bread, a rock pot creation that brings together the heartiness of beans, the freshness of tomatoes, and the comforting touch of bread. This simple yet flavorful soup is a tribute to traditional home cooking, offering a warm and satisfying meal for any day.

Servings: 6

Prepping Time: 15 minutes

Cook Time: 6 hours (Low heat in Crock Pot)

Difficulty: Easy

Ingredients:

- 2 cups white beans, soaked overnight
- 1 can (14 oz) diced tomatoes
- 1 onion, chopped
- 2 garlic cloves, minced
- 4 cups vegetable broth
- 1 tsp dried basil
- 1 tsp dried oregano
- Salt and pepper to taste
- 4 slices of crusty bread, cubed

Step-by-Step Preparation:

1. Drain and rinse the soaked beans and place them in the Crock Pot.
2. Add diced tomatoes, chopped onion, and minced garlic.
3. Pour in vegetable broth.
4. Season with dried basil, oregano, salt, and pepper.
5. Stir to mix all the ingredients well.
6. Cover and cook on low heat for 6 hours.
7. Before serving, add cubed bread to the soup for added texture.
8. Serve warm and enjoy the hearty flavors.

Nutritional Facts: (Per serving)

- Calories: 210
- Fat: 2g
- Carbohydrates: 40g
- Protein: 12g
- Fiber: 9g
- Sugar: 6g

This soup with beans, tomatoes, and bread celebrates simplicity and taste, perfect for those seeking a wholesome and comforting meal. Its blend of nourishing ingredients and easy preparation makes it a delightful choice for family dinners or a cozy meal on a relaxed evening.

Conclusion

As we conclude "Crock Pot Creations: Culinary Adventures," it's time to reflect on the journey we've embarked upon together. Through 50 recipes spread across five diverse chapters, this cookbook aims to transform your kitchen into a hub of culinary innovation, using only your trusty crock pot.

You've journeyed through chapters dedicated to Meat, Chicken, Vegetarian, Fish and Seafood, and Soup, each offering ten unique and authentic recipes. These dishes, brought to life through vivid, original photography and easy-to-follow instructions, have been designed to cater to various tastes and dietary preferences.

Every recipe in this book has been a testament to the versatility and convenience of crock pot cooking. From the robust flavors of meat dishes to the delicate nuances of vegetarian cuisine and from the hearty warmth of soups to the refined subtleties of fish and seafood recipes, this cookbook has endeavored to cover an extensive culinary spectrum. The full-color printing enhances your experience, ensuring that each dish you prepare is as visually appealing as delicious.

We hope that "Crock Pot Creations" has been a guide and a source of inspiration for you. The perfect blend of flavors, the ease of cooking, and the joy of sharing these meals with loved ones are the experiences we aim to bring into your home. The satisfaction of mastering these recipes, each tested to perfection, is a feeling we hope you cherish and continue to explore.

As you continue your culinary adventures, let the lessons and experiences from "Crock Pot Creations" guide you. Experiment with flavors, adapt recipes to your liking, and, most importantly, enjoy the process of cooking. Your feedback and experiences are invaluable; share them with others who might be inspired to begin their journey with a crock pot.

In closing, thank you for allowing "Crock Pot Creations: Culinary Adventures" to be a part of your cooking journey. May your kitchen always be filled with the aromas of delicious food, the warmth of good company, and the joy of creating something extraordinary. Keep cooking, experimenting, and, most importantly, enjoying every bite of your culinary creations!